The PC Parent

PCReview

The PC Parent

*You and your kids
in the age of computers*

Gus Silber

ZEBRA

ZEBRA

Published by Zebra Press
a division of Struik Publishers (Pty) Ltd
(a member of the Struik Publishing Group (Pty) Ltd
32 Thora Crescent, Wynberg, Sandton

Reg. No.: 54/00965/07

First published in September 1997

© Struik Publishers 1997
Text © *Mail & Guardian* 1997

All rights reserved. No part of this publication may be reproduced, stored in a retrieval system or transmitted, in any form or by any means, electronic, mechanical, photocopying, recording or otherwise, without the prior written permission of the copyright owner/s.

All terms referred to in this book that are known to be trademarks or service marks have been capitalised appropriately. Zebra Press cannot affirm the accuracy of this information. Use of terms in this book should not be considered as affecting the validity of any trademarks or service marks.

Editor Sandra Coelho
DTP and cover design Neels Bezuidenhout
Illustrations Anthony Stidolph

Reproduction by Disc Express cc, Johannesburg
Printed and bound by CTP Printers (Pty) Ltd, PO Box 6060, Parow East 7501

ISBN 1 86872 073 X

Dedication

This one's for Sarah Jane, whose first word of more than two syllables was 'kom-pooh-ter'

Acknowledgements

My thanks and salutations to:

Irwin Manoim, the publisher of *PCReview* and all-round computer whizz-person. Irwin doesn't know it, but it was his painstaking explanation of the process of copying a file from hard drive to floppy that put me on the road, many years ago, to becoming a total computer nut.
Mish Middelmann, PC parent and fellow author, for his much-valued advice and input.
Arthur Goldstuck, editor of *PCReview*, for inviting and encouraging me to write about kids and computers.
The many people, at home and abroad, who willingly took the time to share their expertise and answer my niggling questions on kids and computing. Their names are scattered throughout this book, which would not have been possible without them.
My wife, Amanda, for her fearless criticism and unstinting support.
Marga Collings, Sandra Coelho and Tamsin Shelton of Zebra Press for somehow putting up with me and my book.
PC parents and computer kids everywhere. You've been an inspiration.

Contents

Part One: Getting Started

Chapter 1:   Ag pleez, Daddy, can we have a computer?
             Setting out and starting up 13
Chapter 2:   'I can do it all by myself!'
             Introducing kids to computers 26
Chapter 3:   Who's afraid of the big bad mouse?
             The fine art of mousing around 35
Chapter 4:   Don't touch that button!
             Childproofing your PC 42
Chapter 5:   Just when you thought it was safe to use a computer…
             Health and safety hints for PC parents 50
Chapter 6:   The cyber generation
             Talking to kids about computers 55

Part Two: Software

Chapter 7:   So, edutain me!
             How to choose and buy children's software 65
Chapter 8:   Try before you buy — the shareware concept
             How to get great children's software for next to nothing 77
Chapter 9:   Blam! Splat! Whoomph!
             It's only a game 87
Chapter 10: Digital dolls and virtual shopping
             Computers are a girl's best friend 95

Part Three: The Internet

Chapter 11: Sex, drugs, rock'n'roll and the Internet
Is this a nice place to bring up your kids? 103
Chapter 12: 50 weird, wacky and wonderful things for kids
(and their parents) to do on the World Wide Web 115
Chapter 13: How to find out everything you ever wanted
to know about anything on the Internet 127
Chapter 14: A home on the Web
Build a place in cyberspace 148

Part Four: Schools and Computers

Chapter 15: Goodbye, Mr Chips
Computers in the classroom 167
Chapter 16: The wired classroom
Schools and the Internet 175
Chapter 17: The cyberteachers
Blazing a trail on the information highway 180
Chapter 18: The Internet without a net
Putting the Web to work in South African schools 186
Chapter 19: Slacker heaven
The incredible, amazing homework machine 191
Chapter 20: Teach your children
Computers and the homeschool revolution 197
Chapter 21: Computer tutors of the future
The private tuition option 204

How to speak cyber
A handy glossary for the older generation of newbies 215

Index 223

Part One
Getting Started

Chapter 1

Ag pleez, Daddy, can we have a computer?

Setting out and starting up

In the early Eighties, gazing through his nerd-glasses into the not-too-distant future, Microsoft mega-billionaire Bill Gates had a vision of a world in which every family home would be equipped with a personal computer. He was wrong. You need at least two of the things. One for you, one for the kids.

Otherwise, prepare to be wrenched by one of the most agonising dilemmas of contemporary parenting: encouraging your offspring to explore, experiment and go boldly into the New Digital Frontier, while discouraging them from putting their grubby paws anywhere near your precious machine.

In an ideal world, personal computers, like pocket calculators, would be affordable enough to buy in bulk and distribute to every member of the household. We're not there — yet.

A good family computer, equipped with such must-have accessories as a CD-ROM drive (to run the latest multimedia software) and a modem (to hook you up to the Internet) can easily set you back R7 500. That's even more expensive than a deepfreeze. Then again, how many of the following things can you do with a deepfreeze?

- make professional-looking birthday cards, banners, posters and newsletters
- calculate complex algebraical formulas in a flash
- read the latest issue of the *Bahrain Tribune* or the *Hindustan Times* without setting foot outside your door
- scour the shelves of the Library of Congress in Washington for information on South African invertebrates

- send a message to your cousin in Toronto for no more than the cost of a local phone call
- search *The Complete Works of Shakespeare* for all occurrences of the word 'fop'
- plot the movement of comets and satellites in the night sky
- play chess against a ten-year-old grandmaster-in-the-making in Moscow
- explore a Mozart symphony in music, words, notation and pictures
- store food in bulk for months at a time.

Okay — so computers can't do everything. But let's assume you've weighed the pros and cons and balanced the family budget. (Did I mention how easy it is to balance the family budget with a personal computer?) Here's the good news. Barring foreign exchange fluctuations and natural disasters in the Far East's microchip belt, computer prices will continue falling in inverse proportion to advances in computer technology. And here's the bad. Buying a family computer is a process more fraught with pitfalls and confusion than ever before.

The big problem: too much freedom of choice. In the pre-Mesozoic era of personal computing, *circa* 1985, it was all very easy. If you needed a PC at all, and you probably didn't, you strolled into your local 'microcomputer' dealership and said, 'I'd like to buy a computer.' Your choice was simple: IBM or IBM-compatible. Since IBMs were more expensive, you didn't need much persuasion to settle for the Taiwanese clone.

Cobbled together from oddments and off-cuts, it wasn't even graced with a name. But it did belong to a certain species of computer, and that species was called the 'XT'.

XTs were unlovely but robust machines, boasting monochrome screens with shimmering green or orange letters, dual floppy-disk drives, and internal speakers that played digitised music with cellophane-and-comb fidelity. XTs were fine for processing words, doing the books, building a database of your favourite recipes, and playing a version of Space Invaders that left everything to the imagination. Suffice it to say that XTs were not a big hit with the younger generation. But things have changed.

XTs are extinct (hence the name), and computers have become the new rock'n'roll. Imagine a machine that combines your compact-disc player with your television with your library with your telephone with your fax with your video recorder with your accountant with your filing cabinet with the amusement arcade down the road. Small wonder that you're beginning to pick up a strange whining noise in the background: 'Mom? Dad? Can we have a computer?'

Of course, kids. But first, I'm going to give your parents a piece of excellent advice that will assist them in buying the right computer for everybody's needs. Parents! Get hold of a copy of *Buying the Right Computer* by Irwin Manoim, which is one of the companion books in this *PCReview* series.

In the meantime, let's run through some of the nagging questions that may come to mind as you contemplate this life-changing decision. If you already have a powerful multimedia computer with Internet access (or if you already have Irwin's book), feel free to fast-forward through the following bits, and I'll meet you on page 26.

The family computer FAQ

Q: *FAQ? What's a FAQ?*
A: A FAQ (pronounced 'fak') is a list of 'frequently asked questions', such as the one you've just asked. FAQs are common in the computer world and are designed to communicate essential information in an easy-to-read, user-friendly manner.

Q: *Okay. My first question is, should I buy a second-hand computer for my kids? A friend has offered me a '386' model that appears to be in excellent condition. I'm told it was only used by a little old lady to do her bookkeeping on Sundays.*
A: Buying a used computer is a bit like sticking your hand into a jar of live snakes. You could get bitten; then again, the snakes might turn out to be harmless.

In principle, there is nothing wrong with the practice of recycling previously owned computers and components. Computer buffs are forever trading, upgrading and transplanting bits and pieces, and even a cranky old XT may still be perfectly capable of doing the job it was designed to do more than a decade ago.

The trouble is that the 'job' isn't what it used to be. Today's computers are expected to perform a gruelling array of tasks, from digitising sound to manipulating 3-D images to transmitting files and messages across the globe. They need lightning-fast processors, tons of memory and gargantuan hard drives for storing programs and data.

Yesterday's computers usually don't have these things. Which is why people are so keen to get rid of them. To use a random example from my local knock-and-drop, someone is trying to offload a 486 SX-33 computer (that refers to the machine's processing speed, in the same way that '1600' or '1800' refers to the engine capacity of a car) with 8MB of RAM, a 270MB hard drive and an SVGA colour monitor for R1 500 or the nearest cash offer. Sounds like a bargain.

Indeed, you would probably only need to spend another six or seven grand on a new motherboard, processor, CD-ROM drive, extra memory and a bigger hard drive to turn that relic of the distant past into a machine your kids could feel proud of. True, many households compute happily on older, slower computers of the 486 or 386 variety. But the time will surely come when a dealer is unable to repair or replace a defective component, or your trusty workhorse sinks to its knees in the bid to run a vital new piece of software.

Computers are the kamikazes of modern technology, programmed to plunge in value and render themselves obsolete every time a new processor or operating system arrives on the scene.

Today's hero is the multimedia Pentium with Windows 95. Everything else, from the ancient XT to the bargain 486, is for the brave and nostalgic only. Save money. Save aggravation. Buy new.

Q: *I'm confused. I've made up my mind to buy a personal computer for the kids, but a colleague who is an expert on these matters says I should buy them an Apple instead. What's an Apple?*
A: An Apple (full name: Apple Macintosh) is a computer designed for personal use, but it is not a personal computer. That appellation refers strictly to the direct descendants or 'clones' of the original IBM PC that launched the desktop computer revolution in 1981.

Apple Macs came a bit later, and immediately won the hearts and minds of home users, particularly those with children. Suddenly, there was no need to memorise a string of arcane commands for execution at the dreaded DOS prompt. All you had to do was manipulate a graphical input device, sweetly called a 'mouse', and make things happen by 'clicking' on little pictures on the screen.

It would take years for PCs to catch up with this revolutionary notion. In the meantime, the smiley-faced Mac became a working definition of the family-friendly Plug and Play home computer. It still is.

You can buy a complete Mac system off the shelf, connect a few cables, plug it in, and get straight down to work or play. Even an adult can do it. And yet, there are several sound reasons why Macs remain a rarity in the South African home market:

- They're more expensive than PCs, and are less likely to be stocked by your local computer dealer. (Apple's pull-out from South Africa in the mid-Eighties coincided with the rise of the PC, and the company has yet to re-establish itself as a force in the local market).
- Software for the Mac is conspicuously less ubiquitous than software for the PC.
- If your child uses a computer at school, it's more likely to be a PC. It makes sense to use the same format at home.
- Although significant moves have been made towards reconciliation, Macs and PCs remain fundamentally incompatible. Transferring information between them is, at best, a schlepp.
- Thanks to the advent of Microsoft's Windows 95 operating system, PCs are now almost as easy to use as Macs.

In any case, do you really need a computer that smiles at you when you switch it on?

Q: *Yes.*
A: Well, you're in good company. Macs rule in the publishing, advertising and engineering fields, where their combination of raw power and sleek design gives them an edge over even the most powerful PC.

For home use, you'll probably be looking at a Mac in the mid-priced Performa range. Even the plain vanilla models feature built-in stereo sound, internal CD-ROM drives and a generous selection of pre-loaded software, including some fine titles for children.

At the bottom of the range is the Performa 630, which boasts built-in DOS compatibility. Meaning: Unlike other Macs, it's capable of turning itself into a PC and running all those DOS and Windows applications that normally give an Apple apoplexy.

But it's a hybrid solution, with two slower processors adding up to the second-best of both worlds. You may be better off making a firm commitment to one format or the other and, if your choice is Mac, you can't go wrong with the Performa 5200.

It's a compact, if not exactly lightweight machine, with an all-in-one monitor and case built around a zesty 75MHz PowerPC chip. The 5200 comes standard with a 500MB hard drive and 8MB of RAM. You may want to consider doubling both those options if the Mac is to be all things to all members of the household.

Q: *I'm even more confused. The shelves of my local PC hyper are groaning with computer systems, but not one of them is called a 'Pentium'. They all have names like 'Acer', 'Packard Bell', 'Compaq' and 'Fujitsu', except for the ones that don't have names at all.*
A: That's because a Pentium isn't a type of computer. It's a type of computer chip (or 'central processing unit', as they prefer to be called).

If you open up the part of your computer that looks like a vertical or horizontal box — that is to say, the part that isn't a monitor or keyboard — you'll see the Pentium chip sitting there in all its flat, black, biscuit-sized glory. Actually, you won't see it because the Pentium chip is so fast and powerful that it has to be topped by a tiny fan to prevent it from melting the internal organs of your computer.

The Pentium is the part of your computer that actually computes, executing trillions of instructions and transferring reams of information at your supreme command. No wonder kids love these things.

Entire computer systems are designed, built and shipped to market around the Pentium chip, which is available in several different speeds. You'll find a confusing array of brands and configurations, but your choice really comes down to this: clone or brand name?

Q: *Thanks. That helps a lot. So what's the big difference between a clone and a brand name?*
A: A clone is really just a box with components, added or modified to your specifications.

You can have more of this, less of that, a bigger this, and a slightly more advanced version of that. It's the 'Build Your Own Sandwich' philosophy of computer buying. With a brand-name system, the sandwich is already there on the shelf. You just pay your money and take it away.

The catch, of course, is that the fillings — okay, the components — will often have been manufactured in the same US or Far Eastern factories. Processor, hard drive, video card, memory chips — under the hood, all computers tend to look alike.

Still, there are several compelling reasons why you should consider buying a brand-name system, beginning with the fact that they are specifically designed with families and home users in mind.

Q: *Tell me more.*
A: Acer, Compaq, Fujitsu, Packard Bell, IBM. What these and other brand-name systems have in common is a revolutionary factor called 'Plug and Playability'. You take them home, you plug them in, you play. (The term 'play', when it comes to computers, shall henceforth be deemed to be interchangeable with the term 'work'.)

It's a tough market out there, so every brand-name system will go out of its way to make your computing experience as painless and friendly as possible. All vital components will have been pre-installed and configured, the operating system will be up and running, and an impressive library of software titles for the whole family will be ready to be clicked into action.

To make things even easier, built-in 'navigational' software will greet you and show you around from the moment you switch on your machine. On the Packard Bell, for instance, the first thing you see after booting up is a breathtaking image of a 'virtual home', with instant access to such areas as the 'living room', 'kids' space', and — alakazam — the Internet.

Learning curve? Forget it. This is a straight line to computer literacy. As someone who learned to compute the hard way, I can think of only one disadvantage to this hand-holding, user-friendly approach.

One day, something will go wrong — even if it is just a teeny 'General Protection Fault' in Windows 95 — and you will be plunged straight over the precipice into chaos and confusion. If you truly want to master the computer, it helps to have some understanding of the stuff that goes on behind those 'click-me' pictures and soothing American accents.

On the hardware level, you should also be aware that brand-name systems, because of their proprietary design, can be slightly more of a schlepp to repair, service and upgrade than their anonymous-looking clones. You want looks? You want style? You want Plug and Play? Go for a brand name you can trust.

Q: *But brand-name systems are more expensive than clones, right?*
A: Not necessarily. You have to compare Apples with Apples. Sorry — Pentiums with Pentiums. For instance, here's a very nice Auwa system with full multimedia and Internet capabilities. It sells for R6 985. (Of course, this will have changed, probably for the better, by the time you read this.)

A clone system with similar specifications would cost you, according to my computer's calculations, R6 022. Seems like a clear-cut choice, until you look at the Auwa's hidden extras: a range of top software titles worth more than R1 000, plus a month's free subscription to an Internet service provider. The clone doesn't even come with Windows 95. Moral: Look closely at the specifications before you buy.

Q: *What sort of 'specifications' should I be looking for?*
A: Good question. The choice doesn't end with clone or brand name. Although the march of technology has eliminated all earlier processors from the equation, you still have to decide between a several flavours of Pentium, from the 'basic' 166 to the Pentium Pro to the Pentium MMX to the blazingly fast Pentium II.

Choosing a faster chip does not mean your kids will get their homework done any quicker. For everyday applications, a Pentium 166 is plenty fast enough.

It's more important to ensure you have enough memory, measured in megabytes of RAM (Random Access Memory), to run your applications to their full potential. Some discount dealers still sell Pentium systems with 8MB of RAM, but 16MB is the suggested minimum. Otherwise, you'll be driving a Ferrari with a lawnmower engine.

Here are some other things to look out for:

➡ **Secondary cache** A backup form of memory that steps in when your RAM is feeling woozy. Also known as 'Level 2' or 'L2' memory. Most systems have 256 kilobytes on board.

➡ **Hard drive or hard disk** The slim but weighty box that stores your precious data and programs. These build up at an alarming rate, especially if you're sharing a computer with your kids. A 1.2 gigabyte model will give you room to grow. (A gigabyte is a thousand megabytes, a megabyte is a million bytes, and a byte — not to be confused with a bit — is a teeny piece of digital information, such as the full-stop at the end of this sentence.)

➠ **Stiffy drive** Into which you insert stiffy disks, or 1.44MB double-sided high density disks. You'll use them for installing programs, transferring files and backing up your hard drive.

➠ **Monitor** Often overlooked, despite being looked into for hours at a time. Most systems are sold with a 14-inch Super VGA colour monitor, but your eyes will be forever grateful if you can bump that up to 15 inches or 17 inches. Have a good look at the monitor in action, and make sure it's a non-interlaced model with a dot pitch no greater than 0.28 millimetres. Otherwise, put the migraine medication on standby.

➠ **Video card** Also known as a 'graphics card' or 'display card'. This is the internal device that acts as the intermediary between your computer and your monitor, thereby putting you in the picture. The quality of the card will determine the resolution and speed of your display, and will have a direct bearing on the overall performance of your system. You'll need a card with at least 1MB of DRAM or VRAM memory. As the name suggests, VRAM is faster. You may not notice the difference in everyday computing, but wait till you try your hand at one of those spectacularly violent alien shoot-'em-up games that you'll soon be warning your children about.

➠ **Keyboard** The simple yet ingenious device that makes all the difference between using a computer and watching television. Your dealer will generously throw in a '101-key' model (count 'em). But you can also splash out on a fancy variation, such as the Microsoft Natural Keyboard, which looks as if it has been left out in the sun after somebody drove over it with a bulldozer. It is alleged to be 'more natural and ergonomic' to use by people who have just spent R399 on one.

➠ **Mouse** Another vital input device, of particular significance in kids' computing. The standard two-button model will do nicely. Gadget freaks will be pleased to know that you can also buy cordless models, three-button models, programmable models, upside-down models and infrared models that look and feel just like a TV remote-control.

Q: *What's all this stuff I keep hearing about 'multimedia'? Do I really need one of those CD-ROM drive things? I've heard they can play music while you work, but I prefer listening to the radio.*
A: More than anything else, the outbreak of multimedia has been responsible for turning otherwise well-adjusted children into computer fanatics. The addition of sound, music, animation and video has turned yesterday's dumb terminal into an all-singing, all-dancing, information, education and entertainment station. And it's all the fault of CD-ROM.

The digital compact disc was originally designed as a nifty replacement for the black vinyl long-playing record, a blow to the spirit from which rock'n'roll has never recovered. But there has been a positive trade-off, thanks to the discovery that CDs can also store up to 650MB of data in a variety of forms.

I have in my possession a CD that contains the full text of 2 000 classic books, including the Bible, the *Complete Works of Shakespeare*, all of Ibsen's plays, and *War and Peace* by Tolstoy. I must get around to reading it someday. But it's when you combine all those media that things really start jumping.

Games, encyclopaedias and children's 'edutainment' titles rely heavily on multimedia, and even the most mundane software packages are routinely distributed on CD to save you having to load 70 stiffy disks in succession. So yes, you do need one of those CD-ROM drive things.

Most family PC systems are sold with CD-ROM drives as standard, or you can choose from one of many 'easy to install' upgrade kits. The drives are rated according to the speed with which they can transfer and access data, beginning with quad-speed and zooming all the way up to 24-speed. (There'll probably be a 48-speed model on the market by the time you read this.)

For now, even a 6X drive is more than sufficient since most multimedia software is designed with the quad-speed standard in mind. You'll also need a sound card to experience multimedia at its most mind-boggling. Make sure it's at least a 16-bit model, and that it is a Sound Blaster or Sound Blaster compatible.

Your sound card will usually come with a little microphone and a pair of low-wattage stereo speakers. There's not much you can do with the microphone other than talk to people on the Internet and record yourself burping. But it's part of the deal, so don't complain.

Q: *The Internet. I'm sure I've read about that somewhere. What do I need to 'get connected'?*
A: Aside from a subscription to an Internet service provider (ISP), what you'll need is a modem. This is a pocket-sized device that allows your computer to engage in a meaningful relationship with your telephone.

You'll be able to send and receive faxes, do your banking, and communicate with friends and strangers all over the world. Actually, you won't because your kids will be too busy looking at stuff on the Internet. We'll explore this topic in more detail later. Let's get back to the modem. Once again: choices, choices.

You can go for an internal or external model, the chief differences being that internal is cheaper, and external offers a reassuring display of blinking lights as it perches on top of your computer. Modems transmit data in kilobytes per second or kps. You'll need a 28.8 or 33.6kps model.

If your computer system has a modem pre-installed, you're in luck, because they're probably the most confounding and temperamental peripherals ever invented. The consolation is that once you've got the thing set up and connected, you'll be able to ask someone on the Internet what you were doing wrong.

Q: *Thanks. I was wondering if you could quickly run those specs by me again so I can photostat the page and show it to my dealer.*
A: No problem. The dream family PC system:
- Pentium processor, 166MHz
- 256kb L2 cache
- 16MB RAM
- 2GB hard drive
- 1.44MB stiffy drive
- 1MB PCI VGA card
- 14-inch 0.28 SVGA non-interlaced monitor
- 101 keyboard

- Microsoft compatible mouse
- 6X or 8X CD-ROM drive
- 16-bit Sound Blaster compatible sound card with stereo speakers
- 28.8 or 33.6kps modem
- a whole lot of free software, or a generous cash discount.

Q: *Can you believe this? I've just bought a dream family PC system for myself and the kids, and now I find I have some money left over on my overdraft. Can you recommend any other items I might need?*
A: Certainly. How about:

- **A colour inkjet printer** Once only fit for printing out a pale imitation of your three-year-old's computer doodlings, these cartridge-based items have improved dramatically in quality and plunged significantly in price. The best models offer crisp, quick-drying printouts of text and images, with near photo-realistic resolution. Now, at last, your three-year-old's computer doodlings will look as garish as nature intended.
    Best brands: Hewlett Packard, Leximark, Epson.
    Cost: about R2 000.

- **A flatbed scanner** With the boom in home computing, colour image scanners have moved out of the repro houses and into the, um, houses. A flatbed scanner is about the size and shape of a photostat machine, and connects to your computer by means of an internal card. You'll find dozens of uses for this amazing device, from copying business cards to 'reading' documents to converting your daughter's high school diploma into an e-mail attachment for Granny in Toronto.
    Best brands: Hewlett Packard, Mustek, Umax.
    Cost: about R2 200.

- **A joystick** A joystick is a digital input device, consisting of a solid base, a flexible, contoured lever, and buttons in the vicinity of your thumb and index finger. It is used for destroying enemy aircraft, blowing Cyborg warriors to smithereens, and developing your child's hand-eye co-ordination. Come on — don't hog the thing to yourself all day.

Best brands: Logitech WingMan, Microsoft Sidewinder 3-D.
Cost: about R500.

➠ **A removable storage device** Backing up computer files is like flossing teeth. Everyone knows you're supposed to do it, but most people can't be bothered. Speak to your dentist about flossing, and get an Iomega Zip 100 drive for your computer. This very cool and blue peripheral, a cinch to transport and connect, accommodates pocket-sized disks that can hold up to 100MB of data. Use for backing up, or give each member of the family a separate disk to store their favourite programs and files.
Best brand: Iomega Zip 100
Cost: about R1 000.

➠ **An uninterruptible power supply** Your kid, the computer genius, has just spent three-and-a-half hours on a multimedia slide-show presentation for tomorrow's Junior Science Seminar. Suddenly, a kitchen appliance trips, and the house is plunged into darkness. Bye-bye scholarship. Avoid the trauma and embarrassment by connecting your computer to a battery-powered UPS, which will provide up to 15 minutes of emergency electricity in the event of an outage or power failure.
Best brands: APS, Mercer.
Cost: about R700.

Q: *Got it. Just one more question. What am I supposed to do with all this stuff?*
A: Let's find out.

Chapter 2

'I can do it all by myself!'

Introducing kids to computers

Ta-daaaaa!

Four in the morning in a formerly sleepy household in Randburg, Gauteng. Nicky Monzeglio, computer graphics designer, sits up with a start. She's heard that sound before.

As she tries to place it in the darkest hour before the dawn, she becomes aware of a soft blue glow filtering through the house. In the distance, a faint tap-tap-tap. Then a click.

Nicky looks across at her husband. He's fast asleep. That leaves only one possibility. As the fanfare gives way to a jaunty musical theme and a high-pitched word of welcome, Nicky gets out of bed and tiptoes down the corridor. Just as she suspected.

Standing in the doorway, arms folded, Nicky wonders whether to laugh or sigh as she watches her four-year-old daughter installing a CD-ROM and manipulating a mouse without the slightest trace of fear or hesitation.

Meet Daniela Monzeglio, computer nut. Her eyes light up. She smiles and waves hello. Not at her mother, but at the teddy bear on the screen. Ta-daaaaa! Nicky sighs. Just the other day, Daniela figured out how to double-click the icon that connects the family computer to the Internet.

Already, despite the fact that she is a pre-literate pre-schooler, she knows how to delve deep inside a directory and select the executable file that will set-up or start-up a program. How long will it be before she takes over the computer graphics design business?

In the cold light of day, Nicky puts her foot down. She's happy that her daughter is so at home with the educational and occupational tool of the future. She's thrilled that Daniela has so cheerfully mastered the basics of personal computing. She's impressed with the way Daniela has been motivated to explore advanced navigation and file management techniques on her own.

But somewhere, the line must be drawn. Nicky moves the computer out of the bedroom, enables access-control by password, and bans Daniela from using it altogether. Later, she relents. Daniela will be allowed to use the computer for an hour a day, under strict parental supervision. The rest of the time, she must just be herself. A typical, everyday four-year-old.

'I just think,' says Nicky, 'that there has to be more to being a child than sleeping, eating, drinking and talking computers 24 hours a day. I want my daughter to be comfortable with computers. But I also want her to be out there, playing and having fun. Being a boffin can wait for later.'

There are two big lessons to be learned from this little tale of modern family life. The first is that it is no great challenge for kids as young as three or four to learn how to use a computer without supervision. The second is that computers have a role to play in child development. But that role, ideally, should not be played when you are trying to get some sleep at four in the morning.

It is a question of balance. We leave Daniela now and journey to the home of Ed Rybicki, an Associate Professor of Microbiology at the University of Cape Town.

Ed is sitting at his computer, engaged in a deadly serious academic pursuit. Hunting down enemy aircraft in Wing Commander II. Blam! Doof-doof-doof! Ker-blooooiiiieee! As fiery fighters spiral from the sky, Ed recalls with fondness the days when his co-pilot was small enough to fit on his knee.

Now Steven (5) flies solo missions as he notches up the skills that will prepare him for school and adulthood. Taking his pick from his private library of CD-ROMs, he decides for himself what to play, when and for how long. As long as he's learning, as long as he's having fun, Dad's happy.

'He learned to count from a DOS game,' boasts Ed, 'and he learned his alphabet from the CD-ROM version of *Dr Seuss's ABC*. He learned to type his name and several other things from playing games. But we make sure that he spends time with books and pens and paper as well as the computer. The activities complement each other.'

Then again, sometimes Steven wants to do nothing more with his free time than kid around on a jungle gym. Blam! Doof-doof-doof! And so on. It's safe to assume that some of his playground pals won't even have computers at home, while those who do may not quite have mastered the art of sliding a CD-ROM into a drive and double-clicking their way to early academic glory.

Should their parents be alarmed? Should they chastise themselves for depriving their children of a head start in a fiercely competitive job market? Probably not. For all the wonder and excitement associated with personal computing, it pays to remember that Albert Einstein never used a PC. Pablo Picasso never painted with a mouse. And Thomas Alva Edison got along just fine, despite the fact that he never even had an electric lightbulb in the house.

A computer is capable of many marvels, from calculating your bank balance to driving a buggy on Mars to beating Gary Kasparov at chess. But it is not a magic totem. It does not automatically confer genius or success on anyone who masters its fundamentals.

It will not turn a child into a better thinker.

It will not turn a child into a more efficient and productive worker.

It will not take the place of a bedtime story, a set of wax crayons or a 99-cents bottle of bubble-mix.

It will not even be able to tell the difference between something as simple as 'its' and 'it's' when performing a check on your spelling.

So why, then, would you want to introduce your child to one? Well, first of all, it probably won't do any harm. (Just keep those fingers away from those cables.) Secondly, used the right way, with the right software, for the right reasons, a computer just might turn your child into a better thinker and a more efficient and productive worker after all.

But the real reason is simpler still. Children and computers were made for each other. They seem to enjoy a special relationship, an instant connection that is both mystical and mystifying to the average technophobic adult. Even very young kids are unafraid of computers, for the same reason, I suspect, that they are unafraid of dinosaurs.

Logic dictates that a toddler should run screaming in terror from the jaws of a *Tyrannosaurus rex*, or at least a scale model thereof. Doesn't happen. Kids are crazy about dinosaurs. And kids are crazy about computers.

They're unburdened by pre-conceptions, insecurities or the baggage of generations of evolution from the analogue to the digital age. They've never had to listen to a scratched vinyl record, watch a home movie on a Super 8 projector, or imagine a world without cellphones and satellite television. They're at home and at ease in a world of incredible machines.

Shame. One day, no doubt, they'll be telling their children how tough life was in the days of the Pentium 166. For now, put them in front of a computer, and they're flying.

'My kid's a genius!' a parent might exclaim, as the kid casually clicks, connects and makes things happen on a computer screen. Let's give parental pride the benefit of the doubt. But the fact is that today's computers, with their multitasking capabilities and Graphical User

Interfaces, are more powerful, more forgiving and easier to use than ever before.

That's why even an adult, with a little patience, a positive attitude and a four-year-old close at hand, will generally be capable of attaining computer literacy in a matter of weeks. Don't let your kids wait that long. By the time they're adults, there won't even be such a thing as computer literacy; the very notion of literacy will encompass the ability to compute.

Your challenge, as a parent, will not be to introduce your child to your computer. Your challenge will be to get some time on the computer to yourself. With that in mind, let's get down to basics.

Make the computer part of the family

Learn from the experience of Daniela's sleep-deprived mum. Place the family computer in a part of the house where it can be accessed and used by the whole family. This will cut down on sibling rivalry and inter-generational conflict, and will also spare you the trauma of wondering whether your teenage son is really doing his homework behind that closed bedroom door, or whether he is merely looking for pictures of 'babes' on the Internet.

Don Sleeth, a computer programmer and Web site designer from Ottawa, Canada, says the location of a computer can make all the difference to a child's interest in computing.

When his daughter, Nicole, was four years old, 'she really had no desire to play on the computer, and would never do so on her own. I thought it would help if she had her own computer, so I set up a hand-me-down in my basement office. But whenever she wanted to play on it, I would be busy or not in the office. She didn't want to sit there on her own.'

Solution: Don moved the computer to the kitchen.

'We set up a desk for her, and she began playing around on the computer while we were preparing meals, or whatever. Using the computer became an activity for the whole family.'

Today Nicole (10) is herself an accomplished computer programmer, with her own home page on the Internet. Remember: location, location, location.

Learn the art of laptop computing

Frequently asked question: 'When will my child be old enough to learn how to use a computer?' Frequently questioned answer: Whenever your child is old enough to get in the way while you are trying to use a computer.

Infants as young as six or eight months will be instantly attracted by the pretty pictures on the screen, and the irresistible bashability of keyboards and other input devices. Toddlers from about a year on will begin imitating parents and making the vital connections between input and output.

From the terrible twos, kids will be ready to explore on their own — albeit not unattended — and will be capable of manipulating a mouse and asking endless questions of a technical nature. Kids aren't afraid of computer jargon, so use correct terminology when replying.

'This is a floppy drive.' 'This is a CD-ROM.' 'This is an external modem.' 'This is a General Protection Fault in kernel32.dll. Whoops.'

Give constant feedback and encouragement

One of the reasons kids are so comfortable with computers is the fact that computers are so tolerant of kids.

Unlike even the most caring parents and teachers, computers never lose their cool, roll their eyes or slide into dark sarcasm when you pick the wrong answer from a multiple choice.

Instead, computers shower you with praise, feedback and encouragement, and gently guide you back on track when you find yourself heading in the wrong direction. Follow their example, add the personal touch, and you, your kid and your computer will be an unbeatable team.

Resist the temptation to turn your computer into a surrogate television

Great computing myth: It is better for a child to sit in front of a computer than to slouch in front of a television. Fact is, neither activity is inherently good or bad. It depends entirely on the program.

A child can learn just as much about life from watching a video of *The Lion King* as from watching *Just Grandma and Me* on the PC. The big difference with computers is that they offer the option of interaction. So interact.

Sit with your kids, click everywhere on the screen, explore the software together. Before long, the day will come when your kid is confident enough to interact with the computer alone, and you can go off and watch *Egoli* in private.

Offer a menu of alternative activities
Although some kids will turn computing into a four-in-the-morning obsession, the majority will know well enough when to call it a day. They'll compute for an hour or so, get bored, watch TV, read a book, do a puzzle, go out and play.

Geared to individual ages and attention spans, equipped with enough software to build and maintain interest, the computer should be a balanced part of a child's daily menu. Not the whole cake.

Invest in a bashable computer accessory
Given the vast potential market, it's a little surprising that computer designers haven't come up with a computer designed for kids. Then again, maybe it's not that surprising; computers aren't bicycles, and most kids will zoom along happily without training-wheels.

But if you're looking for a device that will save a little wear and tear on your own computer keyboard, here's some advice: get your kid a Comfy.

Equipped with big, bright buttons imprinted with friendly faces, the Comfy Keyboard (Comfy Interactive) comes complete with a lime-green roller at the top and a fire-engine-red telephone receiver on the side. That's how you tell it apart from your own keyboard.

You load up the software, plug the Comfy into a parallel port, and — *voilà!* — you've got yourself an Interactive Electronic Babysitter. Here's how it works. Switch on the keyboard, and five perpetually smiling characters — Buddy the bear, Jumpy the dog, Feely the elephant, Snaily the snail and Comfy the, er, human — invite your child to bash the buttons and direct the action as they set out on their interactive adventures in ComfyLand.

Well, maybe 'adventures' is too strong a word here. The makers of the Comfy, an Israeli educational software company, take pains to assure parents that the animated stories involve no 'violence, destruction, hostility, competitiveness or pain'. *Doom* this ain't. Instead, in child education-speak, the five stories are designed to reinforce positive social values, develop motor and sensory skills, and encourage response to aural and visual stimuli.

Here's the plot: the elephant has a birthday party, and your kid is invited. After cake and the birthday song, it's time for a little motor-skill development. See those five buttons with the friendly smiling faces on the left of your keyboard? Good. Press one, and the birthday buddy of your choice will tell you a story.

Pick the dog, and you get the one about the day Comfy and Jumpy went to the zoo and saw a lion with his paw caught in the bars. Quick! Interaction, please! At the straight-to-camera suggestion of the animated characters on-screen, your child is encouraged to pick up the telephone and call the ever-diligent Snaily to the rescue.

Most toddlers agree that the telephone is one of the greatest children's toys ever invented, so the inclusion of a fully functional model on the Comfy Keyboard is nothing short of a stroke of genius.

Okay, so you can't get an outside line, but you can call any of the characters at the slightest whim, and it really does ring and they really do answer. Leave the phone off the hook, and you even get a genuine human voice politely requesting you to replace the receiver. Thus are life's vital little lessons learned.

As the stories progress, your button-bashing child learns to bring a variety of non-violent crisis situations to a speedy resolution in the usual manner: by changing the weather, changing the colour of natural objects, or getting a speaking animal on the line.

Along the way, such valuable concepts as 'red', 'purple', 'day', 'night' and 'rain' are craftily communicated, while the child is enveloped in a concept of even greater value for our age: if you hit the buttons on an input device, things start happening on a screen. And we're not just talking about the TV remote-control.

But the really great thing about the Comfy Keyboard is the way it encourages spontaneous, non-linear interaction by easily bored toddlers. At any point, the storyline can be interrupted by telephoning a character (they'll thank you for the call, chat briefly and return to the plot), hitting one of the six colour buttons, playing one of the four musical instruments, or rolling the green roller to produce random noises and visual effects.

In this way, the interaction never stops, and your child is momentarily freed from the subtle pressures of politically correct conditioning (the parents' booklet proudly points out that Buddy the Bear does his own cooking, thereby avoiding any gender stereotyping). Either way, this is a wonderful combination of hardware and software, a handy antidote to television, and a giant leap on the long road to computer literacy.

And on that entirely unsolicited note, let's take a closer look at a tiny computer device that has been known to reduce even the most well coordinated adults into a state of fumble-fingered ineptitude.

Chapter 3

Who's afraid of the big bad mouse?

The fine art of mousing around

I stand back from the computer, arms folded, a beam of fatherly pride spreading across my face. It is a haul-out-the-video-camera moment. A milestone of child development, right up there with the first step, first tooth, first word.

I haul out the video camera and press Record. My daughter has just clicked her first mouse.

The cursor darts wildly across the screen, slips off the edge, comes to rest on the cat sitting on the gatepost. Click. The cat leaps into the air, claws desperately at flapping wings, and lands splash on its back in the birdbath. Sarah Jane squeals with delight and applauds the ingenuity of her hand–eye co-ordination. She's only two.

Okay, two-and-a-half. All right, then, almost three. The point is she's made the magical connection between cat and mouse, and taken the first bold step on the road towards an interactive relationship with the personal computer.

Up to this point, she was a willing victim of the plonk-and-watch approach favoured by parents with other chores on their mind. Plonk the kid in front of the PC, fire up the software, let her watch.

Thankfully, the program in question, Mercer Mayer's *Just Me and My Dad* (Little Critter goes on fishing trip with Big Critter), has a Read option that allows you to take the easy way out. But the Play option is what the program is really about.

Exploring, discovering, interacting, opening up a world of sights and sounds. Trouble is, you need a mouse to get there. And learning to use a mouse is like learning to ride a bicycle. Even grown-ups fall off.

36   THE PC PARENT

Some, wounded by the experience, abandon this most common of computer peripherals altogether. Not because they are unable to master the basics of point-and-click, but because they prefer to focus their energies and attention on the 101 keys on a typical computer keyboard.

The rest of us are more than happy to risk getting Carpal Tunnel Syndrome (a painful ailment caused by too much wrist-flicking and finger-clicking) for the freedom and flexibility of an arrow on a screen.

Try surfing the Internet without it. Or using a graphics program. Or getting the cat to fall in the bath. Indeed, so many children's programs are mouse-driven that running them without one would be like watching television without a remote-control. But forget television for a moment.

Let's get interactive.

Click here to continue

Mouseability. To coin a word, it's the ability to manoeuvre and manipulate a graphics-based input device in order to perform actions on a computer screen.

As many grown-ups will testify, you're never too old to pick up this elementary skill. But can you be too young? Debate rages over the minimum age for introducing a child to the notion that mice can have buttons rather than ears, rollerballs rather than feet, and cables rather than tails.

Some parents claim success with toddlers as young as 12 months. We'll give them the benefit of the doubt.(Can it be long before the first proud mom claims to have bred a computer whizzkid by rolling a mouse over her stomach during pregnancy?)

In the real world, two is probably a better age to start mousing around. By that stage, in a typical techno-literate household, the child will have already made the discovery that fingers on buttons can change pictures on television, or — even more exciting — set off a piercing noise that has men in uniform clambering over walls.

But don't panic if your toddler is less successful, or even less interested, in clicking the buttons that make things happen on a computer screen.

In my case, I was quite happy to leave my daughter in the company of the surrogate television, chipping in occasionally to double-click an icon or change a CD-ROM.

Then, one day, her attention wandering during the umpteenth retelling of *Just Grandma and Me*, Sarah Jane picked up the soap-shaped object on the side of the computer and said: 'What's this?'

'A mouse,' I replied. A peal of dismissive laughter.

'No, it's not!' So I set out to prove it.

Mouse aerobics

Teaching mouseability to a toddler takes endless time and patience. Even when the basics of cursor control have been mastered, you've still got the fine skills of double-click, right-click and click-and-drag to contend with. You may begin to wonder why these awkward devices were ever invented.

On a typical two-button mouse, tiny fingers will click the right button at the wrong time, as opposed to the left button at the right time.

The cursor will constantly disappear. The mouse will be moved in wide, reckless circles, instead of narrow, controlled circles. Then, one day, everything will suddenly click into place.

It's a process of serendipitous discovery that can be considerably lightened if you have the right program on-screen. I highly recommend anything in the Living Books series of CD-ROMs.

Based on hard copy classics by such all-time faves as Aesop, Mercer Mayer and Dr Seuss, these pioneering point-and-click hybrids use spoken text and animation to add a new dimension to familiar tales.

Clicking on almost any object in any frame rewards the clicker with a sight gag that never fails to produce a chuckle or a cheer. A starfish launches into a tapdance, a conch shell parps a mean sax solo, a chicken clucks his way through a stand-up comedy routine.

Result: The kid clicks with the characters and the story, and learns a valuable new motor skill into the bargain. But clicking's not the problem. When the screen is crammed with clickable objects, even the most random volley is bound to hit some of the targets some of the time.

Learning to move the mouse to a set location requires more patience, and this is where your guiding hand comes into the picture. Without compromising your child's spirit of independence — there's something about a mouse that turns even the tamest toddler into a control freak — try the 'shift-and-lift' method of mouse mobility.

Put your hand on your child's hand, point at the cursor and shift the mouse just a little in the desired direction. Then lift the mouse, plonk it back where you started and shift again. And again, and again.

When the cursor is where you want it to be — in some programs, it changes shape to let you know you're on target — let go of the mouse, take a deep breath and click the button firmly with your index finger.

No slipping, no sliding. Guaranteed. And if that doesn't work, you're welcome to try the following patented solution.

Don't just click it, Prestik it

In the vast field of children's interactive software, one of the most incredible and amazing titles has to be Dorling Kindersley's *My First Incredible, Amazing Dictionary*.

Each word — in a vocabulary of more than 1 000 — is pronounced, defined and brought to life through zany sound and animation. And one of the best features is a little icon labelled 'Surprise Me'.

Click on it, wait for the drum roll, and you'll be surprised by the words and pictures that pop up on screen. But what if your aim isn't true enough to hit that tiny target every time? You'll just be frustrated.

Worse, you'll be forced to hand over your hard-won possession of the mouse to some interfering adult. So here's what to do about it, adults.

Affix a thin strip of Prestik to the underside of the mouse, taking care not get any in the way of the little grey ball. Place the mouse on the mousepad — you do, of course, have a mousepad — and manoeuvre the cursor until it hits the spot.

Press hard on the mouse. Make it stick. Now let the kid click to its heart's content, and return to what you were doing before you were interrupted.

Works for me.

Kid mice

When you splashed out on your brand-new, family-friendly multimedia PC, the shape, size and quality of the attached graphical input device was probably the last thing on your budget.

Not surprising, since most dealers are generous enough to throw in a generic two-button mouse of the variety that breed like mice in Far Eastern factories.

And for the most part, the common-or-garden mouse will adequately serve your present and future needs. But if you aim to ease the process of interactive education, it's worth bearing in mind that not all mice are created equal.

You don't need to go as far as spending R500 on the Rolls-Royce of computer mice: a four-button Kensington with programmable functions and the kind of styling that looks like it belongs in the Museum of Modern Art.

But an investment in any of the following kid-friendly peripherals could go a long way towards taking the strain out of mousework:

Microsoft Home Mouse While not specifically aimed at kids, the smaller shape and bigger buttons on this device are sure to be a hit with younger users. It comes in a fetching shade of blue, and if you look closely at the buttons and cable housing, you'll see they're shaped like a chimney-topped home, with the cable trailing off as smoke. Too cute.

Microsoft EasyBall You can't miss with this one. It's based on the revolutionary 'trackball' principle of mouse design, according to which the mouse turns turtle and stays in one place, while you go places by rotating the ball.

The enormous ball is an eye-popping yellow, with a single, blue button prominently placed on the perimeter. The idea is that you use both hands to control the mouse, one on the button and one on the ball, a technique which allegedly requires 'less fine-motor control' and makes the cursor infinitely easier to position.

The EasyBall is aimed at children between two and six years old, and its exaggerated dimensions seem to inspire an awesome sense of power. Catching sight of that big yellow ball, my daughter shoves aside her regular mouse and demands: 'I want to press the sun again.'

PC Pals Mouse 'n House Like the Little Bear's chair in the Goldilocks story, this kid-sized mouse feels just right, thanks to its solid grip and comfortable indentations on the three big buttons. Even adults will appreciate its easy-clicking, smooth-rolling performance, although they might be slightly intimidated by the graffiti-covered blue-and-yellow design.

Logitech Kidz Mouse Probably the most ergonomic and fun-to-use kidz mouse on the market, with swish Swiss styling and one big button to banish clicking confusion. Only problem is that it only works with an Apple Macintosh. Some computers have all the fun.

Scan the accessory shelves of your neighbourhood computer store and you'll also find mice with ears and whiskers, mice with flashing lights, mice with their internal organs exposed, and mice cleverly disguised as cheeseburgers. Such items make cool birthday gifts for the computer kid in your life.

But will they make it any easier for a kid to use a mouse? Probably not. They'll just make it more fun. Here are some tips with the former aim in mind.

Top tips for trouble-free mousing
Keep the mouse squeaky-clean Dust, grime and sticky fingers can interfere with a mouse's delicate mechanism, turning a quick click into

a long haul. But don't give the whole mouse a bath: Just clip out the rollerball, wash in warm water, and allow to dry before slotting back in place.

Fine-tune the mouse's motor-skills If the cursor seems to be speeding away from your child, it may be because the software is set for racetrack conditions. In Windows 3.1 or 95, double-click on the mouse icon in Control Panel, and adjust speed and response time to suit your child's reflexes.

Put a trail on the mouse's tail If your child has difficulty keeping track of that teeny little arrow, improve the odds by adding ghostly 'trails' to its tail. Originally intended to improve cursor visibility on passive-colour laptop screens, this kid-friendly option can be selected under 'Mouse Properties' in the Windows Control Panel.

Jazz up the cursor By default, a mouse cursor is a little arrow when it's flitting freely around the screen, and a little hourglass when it's waiting for the computer to compute. Make mousing more fun by transforming that yawnsome cursor into anything from a fish to a frog to an actual, twitchy-nosed rodent. Windows 95 includes a fine selection of animated cursors, or try the options under your mouse's proprietary software in Windows 3.1.

Button-down the appropriate button Most PC mice have two buttons. The left button is for general-purpose clicking and double-clicking; the right button is for opening up a new range of menu options, primarily in Windows 95. In almost all software aimed at children, the left button is the one that makes things happen. Avoid confusion by marking it with a small but bright sticker of your kid's favourite cartoon character. Then, instead of yelling: 'The left button! The left button!' you'll just have to say: 'Click on Pumbaa.'

Chapter 4

Don't touch that button!

Childproofing your PC

Children enjoy to play on computers. But sometimes, children become guerilla, attack and destract computers. Know damage report, make counterplan, and enjoy peaceful computer life.
　　　　　　　　　Advice from a Japanese father's home page
　　　　　　　　　　　　　　　on the World Wide Web

A small fire once broke out at a computer store just up the road from where I stay. No one was injured, and the fire brigade arrived in good time to stop the flames from spreading. But for weeks afterwards, pride of place in the display window was taken by a computer that had borne the brunt of the blaze. It was not a pretty sight.

The keyboard was a mass of twisted gibberish, the tower box was streaked with soot and grime, and the monitor was encased in waves of melted gloop.

But the computer was working. Perfectly.

Pretty pictures danced across its display, beside a sign that warned: 'Don't try this at home!' I would like to second that emotion.

Computers, for the most part, are sturdy beasts of burden. You wouldn't want to throw one down a stairwell, but they do have an almost uncanny ability to survive mechanical catastrophe. Fire, lightning, earthquakes, secondary tobacco smoke … you name it, computers just blink, reboot and get on with their lives.

And yet, there is one force of nature that has the power to prove their undoing. If you have ever seen chocolate smeared over a monitor, Zoo biscuits jammed into a stiffy drive, or strawberry soft drink sloshed over a keyboard, you will know exactly who I am talking about.

No virus yet invented has the potential to devastate a computer as effectively as a kid armed with the right combination of foodstuffs and natural curiosity. See it from their point of view: Every other household appliance has *'Don't touch'* written over it in big, bold letters.

Children instinctively know — or soon get the drift — that they must not fiddle with the buttons on a dishwashing machine or attempt to insert shiny discs into Daddy's new CD player. But when the major household appliance happens to be a multimedia computer, such behaviour is not only allowed, it's actively encouraged.

If you want your children to learn to use computers with confidence, you can hardly apply the 'Don't touch' rule here. But you can lay down certain guidelines. For peace of mind, the integrity of your hardware and software, and all-round harmony in the household, *do* try these at home:

Supervise younger children As tempting as it may be to plonk a toddler in front of a PC with a program running, anything can happen when a dwindling attention-span gives way to the desire to experiment. Spontaneous interaction has its place in computer education, but a sudden high-pitched whine or strangulated gurgle coming from the computer room can really ruin your day. Especially when you discover that it isn't your toddler making the noise.

Button down the basics Most PC systems feature three prominent buttons on the front panel of the boxy bit. Prodding these buttons at inappropriate moments can produce, as the manuals so delicately put it, 'unexpected results'.

It's a proud moment for any parent when a budding computer boffin learns to power up a computer 'all by myself'. But the Power button (or switch) should not be pushed into the off position until the system has completely shut itself down.

Otherwise, data may disappear, drives may crash and harsh words may pollute the air.

It's also a good idea to steer young fingers clear of the button marked Reset. As the name suggests, this is an emergency button that boots your computer back to life when it refuses to respond to any combination of key-presses, mouse-clicks or shouted commands. Pressing Reset when the computer is behaving normally can leave it feeling very confused.

The third button is perhaps an even greater source of confusion to many computer users. Pressing Turbo will not, as you might suspect, make your computer go faster. It will make it go slower. This is to allow today's faster computers to run yesterday's slower games and applications. But why on earth would anyone want to do that?

If your kids have been using your computer, and you're wondering why it's performing so sluggishly, take a look at the Turbo switch. Is it pressed in? If so, press it out. You'll be back to speed in a flash. Better still, ask your nearest computer expert to disable the Turbo option altogether. You don't need it. And neither do your kids.

Teach disk discipline Whether you're installing a program, running a CD, or backing up precious data, disks are your most indispensable computer companions. They should be treated with care by young and old alike. Especially young.

Today's 3.5-inch 'stiffy' disks are a lot sturdier than the 5.25-inch floppy variety of yore, but they're still vulnerable to heat, dust, cold, grime, liquid, magnetic fields and children.

That sliding metal guard at the top of the disk, with its catapulting, click-me action, can be an endless source of fascination and amusement. Most kids will have little difficulty prising apart the plastic shell to see what lies beneath. Try it yourself. See? That circular sliver of magnetic tape is where your data used to live.

Avoid catastrophe by keeping your disks in a safe place. You can 'write-protect' stiffies against accidental erasure by flicking the little black tab at the back of the disk into the open position. But your best defence is education.

Show your kids what the inside of a stiffy disk looks like, and make a point of demonstrating how difficult they are to put back together before Mom and Dad get home.

If you're worried about your stiffy drive being clogged up with Jelly Tots or bottle-tops, consider masking the mouth with insulation tape or cardboard (the mouth of the drive, that is). Make sure older kids are acquainted with correct disk-insertion procedures. The disks will only go in one way, with the metal tab forward and the label-side up. A satisfying click will confirm the basic principle; you very rarely need to apply brute force to operate a personal computer.

The gentle touch is even more important when it comes to CD-ROMs. Handle by the edges only, store in cases when not in use, place in the drive-tray one at a time, and avoid using as frisbees (although they do make very nice coasters). CD-ROM drives can be among the most pernickety components in your computer.

They will often refuse to read a CD that is only slightly scratched or grubby (you can gently clean the shiny side with a lint-free cloth), and do not take kindly to having their motorised trays prodded or pulled by eager young hands. Teach your children to treat them with respect.

Practise safe computing Every sensible parent knows how important it is to scout the household for potential hazards when a crawling infant evolves into an upwardly-mobile toddler. Don't let the computer room escape your scrutiny.

A falling keyboard may not be quite as lethal as a falling frying-pan, but the same principle of safety first applies. Check that all components are on a level surface and out of harm's way, and think twice before adopting the common practice of placing your computer's tower box on the floor to save desktop space.

Pay careful attention, also, to the placement of such stand-alone peripherals as scanners and printers.

My inkjet printer sits on the top level of a two-level bookcase, a convenient chair-spin away from my computer. But it also happens to be a convenient height for my daughter, who is unable to resist the sound of a printer going about its business. I can't tell you how pleasant it is to return from a phone call and discover 75 freshly printed pages scattered around the room.

And while we're on the subject, right now is also a good time to do something about that awful tangle of cables at the rear of your computer system. Don't wait to see what happens when your toddler gives them a yank. Use cable ties or those newfangled plastic 'sleevelets', available from most computer and electrical outlets.

Don't mess around with magnets Magnets are to computers as green kryptonite is to Superman. Even a simple household magnet, of the variety used to affix finger paintings to fridges, can give your computer a severe attack of amnesia.

Magnets are very good at corrupting or erasing data on stiffy disks or hard drives. But they're even better at playing havoc with your computer's most expensive component — the monitor. That's why the speakers you choose to use with your multimedia computer *must* be of the 'magnetically shielded' type.

It's probably best not to tell your kids that a magnet waved in front of the monitor can leave an interesting array of red and green and purple blotches on the screen. If they do decide to conduct the experiment, try pressing the Degauss button on your monitor's front or rear panel. Otherwise, wait a few days. The blotches should go away.

Say no to foodstuff and spillables Ever wondered what happens to the inner workings of a floppy drive when it is used as a holding bay for a half-eaten lemon cream biscuit?

Ever wondered what happens when a CD-ROM drive tries to read a disk that was last seen in the possession of someone who was eating a toffee apple?

Ever wondered how well a keyboard is able to spell when half a cup of Coke has just seeped into its circuits?

Children don't wonder. Children find out. Make it a hard and fast rule from the start: 'No eating or drinking within 20 centimetres of information technology.' And that goes for chewing gum too.

Liquids can be lethal to computer components. Be sure to set a good example to your children. (I once spilled half a can of Castle Lager over the keyboard of my Olivetti M24. Fortunately, I had a spare close at hand. Too bad about the keyboard.)

You can buy see-through plastic keyboard covers from most computer shops, but if the worst comes to the worst, here's a handy tip: To restore a crumb-filled, cooldrink-stained keyboard to its former glory, wash it with soap and water and hang it on the line to dry. Seriously. Just remember to plug it out first, and make sure it's *completely dry* before you plug it back in. And don't try this with any other piece of computer equipment. Seriously.

Safeguarding your files

Apprentice President George Washington entered the annals of history by confessing that he had, indeed, cut down his old man's cherry tree. Today's youthful felons can stake their claim by admitting: 'I cannot tell a lie, Dad. I accidentally reformatted the hard drive and erased your 1997 budget spreadsheet files.'

These things happen. A key-press or mouse-click in the wrong place, a wander down the wrong directory path. The consequences, for parent and child alike, can be disastrous.

If you share a computer at home, the following precautions, faithfully appplied, could save your child from a fate worse than the American presidency:

Back up, back up, back up! Probably the most often heard and ignored words in the lexicon of personal computing. Having almost recovered from a system crash that wiped out every file on my hard drive (all I was doing was installing an over-zealous new antivirus program), I can confirm that backing up your data regularly is a very sensible idea.

It's not just the horribly silent sound of crashing disks that you have to worry about. A child may innocently erase vital information by, for instance, saving a homework document as PROJECT.DOC, when you've already saved a work-related file under the same name. In an instant, your file will be over-written and unrecoverable. Unless you've got a backup.

Or maybe your child will be idly exploring Explorer on the Windows 95 desktop, when the temptation to fill and empty that cute little recycle bin proves impossible to resist. In a flash, your folders will be in the trash. Unless you have a backup.

Or maybe an evil-minded pal will dare your child to execute a FORMAT C:\ command in DOS. At the press of a 'Y', your drive will be history. Unless you've got a backup.

Use the Microsoft Backup utility included in Windows 3.1 and Windows 95, or invest in an add-on program like Norton Backup for Windows. You don't need to back up your entire drive — just the documents, spreadsheets, images, databases, recipes, homework projects, presentations, system files, agenda entries, address books, e-mail messages and ... okay, maybe you do need to back up your entire drive.

A tape drive or Iomega Zip drive will make the process slightly less of a schlepp, but the ideal — if you have a CD-ROM drive — is to have your system backed up on CD. The special CD-recordable devices that do this are still too expensive for home use, but many computer dealers and consultants will do the job for you at a nominal cost.

Password-protect your files Many everyday applications, from word processors to spreadsheets to home accounting programs, allow you to assign passwords to stand sentry against intruders and inquisitive kids.

The catch is you have to think of a password that isn't so easy that a kid will guess it, and isn't so difficult that you'll forget it. The best passwords contain a random mixture of lower- and upper-case letters and numbers, as in LxV5nQB. (Sorry, you can't use that one. It's mine.)

Although passwords aren't an infallible means of protection — if a 13-year-old hacker can crack the portals of the Pentagon, a home system shouldn't prove too much of a challenge — the message will be delivered loud and clear: this area strictly off-limits.

Make your files Read-Only (not to mention invisible) For added protection against unauthorised editing and modification, save your files as Read-Only. You'll find the option listed under Properties or Save As in almost every program that allows you to work with files. In Microsoft Word, for example, click on File, then Save As, then Options, then Read-Only Recommended.

What this does, as you can probably guess, is allow you to read files but not alter them in any way. The catch? You have to remember to reverse the process every time you feel the need to write as well as read.

What's more, there's nothing to prevent a Read-Only file from being deleted, accidentally or on purpose. There has to be a better way. Here it is: Make your files and folders invisible.

The magic solution is an ingenious little shareware program called Magic Folders, available on the Internet at http://www.pc-magic.com. (If you're not sure what all that means, see Chapter 8 on shareware.) You hide the program in your system, apply it to the folders or directories of your choice and, suddenly, to all intents and purposes, they're not there.

They can't be accessed, modified, viewed, deleted or otherwise tampered with — unless you know the password. Share this program (but not your password) with the kids who share your computer. You can bet they also have a bunch of files they wouldn't want any intefering adult to see.

Chapter 5

Just when you thought it was safe to use a computer...

Health and safety hints for PC parents

Warning! Computing can be hazardous to your children's health. Never mind the horrors of cyberspace, never mind the perils of interplanetary warfare, never mind the effects of pressing the wrong key in the wrong place at the wrong time. The real danger of computing, to children and adults alike, is computing itself.

Slouched in your chair, mesmerised by the monitor's unearthly glow, you peck at the keys and repeatedly click the buttons of an oddly shaped input device. Result? Backache, burning eyes, a pounding head and the slow but painful realisation that your mousing hand is falling victim to Carpal Tunnel Syndrome, the occupational ailment of the Nineties. Now move over and give your kids a chance.

Flush with the joys of watching an infant computer genius executing a perfect double-click, parents can easily overlook the attendant hazards. A toddler tip-toeing on mom's rollaway office chair is an accident waiting to happen, while a teenager in near-horizontal slouch, surfing the Web or blowing aliens apart, is ... well, a teenager.

Sit up straight! Stop slouching! Take your feet off the desk! As my Standard 2 teacher always used to say. She had a point. These days, we call it 'ergonomics', and it's becoming especially important for younger minds to get a grip on what that means: paying attention to the physical aspects of computing rather than just the stuff that's on the screen.

Computing is a sedentary pursuit. To say it exercises the mind rather than the body is to ignore such attractions as Krush Kill 'n' Destroy and the Beavis and Butt-head home page. But it doesn't have to be a dangerous pursuit.

The effects of ergonomically unsound computing may only make themselves felt in later years, but it's never too early to get a fix on the basics.

Some things to watch out for:

Put the computer in its place

The area where the computer resides in your household is amusingly referred to as a 'work station'. (A PlayStation, on the other hand, is an awesomely cool device that hooks up to your monitor and allows you to play high-intensity action games all day long. Slogan: Say goodbye to your life.)

Whether you choose to place the computer and its peripherals on a traditional office desk, a re-commissioned kitchen table or one of those fancy modular work stations you can order by mail, ease of access and comfort of use should be the main criteria.

Computer systems shouldn't be crammed into cubicle-sized corners. You need room to move a mouse, let alone swing a cat. All relevant buttons and drive-bays should be within easy reach of even the youngest of authorised users, and the work surface should be generous enough to accommodate the plentiful accessories associated with computing. But perhaps the most important aspect of proper placement is lighting.

Aim for a good mix of natural and artificial light, and make sure that the sun doesn't shine in your eyes or bounce right off your monitor. If you can see your main source of light reflected in the monitor, then either the monitor or the light is in the wrong place. A combination of fluorescent and incandescent lighting, with a little sunlight on the side, is probably easiest on the eyes.

Invest in a good chair (or two)

A good computer chair from a reputable office equipment store, as opposed to a vendor on the side of the road, can easily set you back more than R1 000. But you'll immediately feel the benefits.

Look for a chair with comfortable-but-not-too-comfortable padding, solid yet flexible support for your back and neck, adjustable swivel-and-tilt movement, armrests to facilitate typing, and all necessary controls to fine-tune height and angle to personal preference.

The problem with a perfect computer chair is that it may not be perfect for every member of the family. Kids on a Goldilocks-style quest for comfort will need their own chair — it's about time someone took the concept of the infant's feeding-chair into the computer age — or cushions for added height and back support. Dangling feet are bad for circulation, so a footstool or small coffee table is also a good idea.

Keep an eye on posture

If you want your kids to grow up as healthy, upright members of the community, encourage good posture from an early age. The following is not good posture: leaning back with keyboard in lap and feet on desk; slumping forward with nose against monitor and joystick in hand; seeing how fast you can spin around in your chair while surfing the World Wide Web; standing in a hunched position over the keyboard because you're in too much of a hurry to sit down; perching on the very edge of the chair to avoid disturbing the cat.

The following is good posture: sitting with your back straight, your shoulders relaxed, your feet on the floor, and your elbows at a 90-degree angle when your hands are on the keyboard. The monitor should be about an arm's length away, and just a little lower than eye level. When you're typing, your fingers should be in a straight line with your forearms. When you're not typing, your hands should be at your side or in your lap.

You should shift your position every 20 minutes or so, just to give your body something interesting to do. Even so, the problem with developing and maintaining good posture, especially as far as kids are concerned, is that it seems to fly in the face of our natural instincts. It's much easier to slack, slouch and slump your way into your personal comfort zone.

But the conscious effort will soon pay off in reduced muscle strain and fatigue, and the lessened risk of Carpal Tunnel Syndrome and other potentially debilitating Repetitive Strain Injuries (RSIs).

In the computing environment, these are usually associated with excessive 'hunt-and-peck' typing, a too-tight grip on the mouse, frenzied clicking, and the mounting pressures of 'static exertion': sitting at your computer, performing precise, controlled, not-very-active movements for hours on end.

The antidote: Get up and do something else.

Take regular breaks

Trapped in the complex maze of an arcade-game underworld, lost in the intricacies of a 3-D animation, hooked on the thread of a live Internet chat, the young computer user can easily lose track of time, space and mind.

Save your kids from becoming computer zombies by reminding them to take 'microbreaks' every three to five minutes, even if it's just to look away from the screen or flex their typing fingers, and active breaks every half an hour or so.

They should get up, stretch, touch the ceiling, karate-kick, grab a bite, drink some water, stare at the moon, talk to a human being, and indulge for a while in such comparatively wholesome activities as listening to heavy metal or watching television. The computer will still be there when they get back. And if they don't follow your advice, maybe the computer won't be there when they get back.

Watch out for eyestrain

Computing can be agony on the eyes. It's easy to see why. Even with today's high-resolution, flicker-free monitors, using a computer puts great strain on your optical muscles.

You're constantly shifting focus between monitor and keyboard, printed document and monitor, monitor and the outside world. Your vision is fixed unblinkingly on one point on the screen, or you're watching a blur of text and images rush by as you hit the scroll buttons.

You're watching an explosion of light and colour from arm's length, or you're peering closer to read yellow text on a blue background on a bright-orange Web page.

A simple fact: If you use a computer for any length of time, sooner or later, you're going to complain about eyestrain. Medical science is divided about the long-term effects, but there's no point in taking chances with younger users.

If you notice your kids squinting or rubbing their eyes at the computer, here's what you can do to lessen the agony:

Install a good anti-glare screen or filter These flip over the face of your monitor, and come in two basic varieties: cheap and not-so-cheap. The cheap variety cut out the glare to a certain extent, but you'll spend most of the time trying to see past your own reflection.

Blink Somehow, the eye forgets to perform this important little exercise while it is glued to the action on a computer screen. Blink rapidly and often to reassure your eyes that the action won't go away.

Refocus Look away from the screen and focus on a distant object every 10 to 15 minutes. This allows the eyes to readjust and relax, and prevents the condition known as 'computer zombie stare'.

Adjust brightness and contrast Fiddle around with your monitor's controls until it looks just right. If it doesn't, buy a better monitor — it's the one computer component you shouldn't cut costs on.

See the optometrist Or is the optician? Whatever, this is especially important if your child wears prescription glasses or contact lenses, not all of which are designed to cope with the burdens of computing. Some eye doctors will prescribe a special brand of 'VDT glasses' called Prio, which have become essential accessories for far-sighted computer nerds around the world.

Chapter 6

The cyber generation

Talking to kids about computers

Our mom doesn't know a single thing about them.
           SHANE (8) AND SASHA (10), COMPUTER KIDS

Saturday morning at the K-Net computer centre in Rivonia, Sandton. Upstairs, in worlds of their own, kids lean forward at their terminals, travelling the Internet, analysing spreadsheets, manipulating digital images. An advanced group clusters quietly round a whiteboard, riveted by the basics of programming in Visual Basic.

Downstairs, sitting round a table in the rest and recreation area, we have: Shane (8) and her sister Sasha (10), Michael (12), Kevin (13) and Paul (14). They've agreed to take a break from the extra-curricular activities at hand to talk about a subject close to their hearts and minds. Let's go...

So, tell me a little about your computers.
SASHA: Me and my sister have got our own computer that we use at home.

Do you ever fight over whose turn it is to use the computer?
SASHA: No, never.
SHANE: Sometimes.
SASHA: No we don't!
MICHAEL: I've got my own computer in my bedroom. I was lucky. I won it in this, like, raffle at K-Net. I've already upgraded it to a Pentium.
KEVIN: I've been using my own computer since I was six. My parents work in computer automation, so they always used to hand me down their old computers. But now I'm using a Pentium 100. Well, not right now, because I've been banned from using it.

What did you do?
KEVIN: I got bad school marks. My parents took my computer away and moved it into their office.

That must be rough.
KEVIN: Ya. But luckily they work from home.

What do you use your computers for?
KEVIN: Games! And other things.
PAUL: Games and school projects.
MICHAEL: Typing, graphics, homework. Games, also.
SASHA: Everything.
SHANE: Games.

What kind of games?
PAUL: Strategy and warcraft. My favourite is *Diablo*.
MICHAEL: My favourite is *Red Alert*.

Do your parents ever complain about the games?
PAUL: No. I think you can learn a lot from strategy and warcraft.
MICHAEL: My dad doesn't mind because he knows the games aren't really real.
KEVIN: I get my cousin to bring his computer to my house, and then we link up with serial cables and play multiplayer shoot 'em ups. My parents don't really mind. Although I do keep the age restrictions hidden.
SHANE: My mother doesn't like a lot of the games. She says they're too violent. I like games where you can go on a quest and find out all sorts of different and nice things.
SASHA: I got a game for my birthday — *Muppet Treasure Island*.
SHANE: No! Not *Muppet Treasure Island!*
SASHA: The one where the Muppets get stuck inside your computer.
KEVIN: I got an upgrade to 16 megs of RAM. But the computer had to get taken to the shop because me and Paul tried to put the chips in by ourselves.
PAUL: Some stupid child threw a piece of Lego into the computer. It got stuck and damaged the chips. We got them in, but it wouldn't work.
KEVIN: I'm not even allowed to open my computer after that.

What do you do when something goes wrong with your computer?
SASHA: 'Da-a-a-a-a-ad!'
SHANE: I know how to use Alt-F4 and Shutdown.

Do your parents ever complain that you're spending too much time on the computer?
PAUL: No. Mine worry about me going on the Internet for a long time.

Are they worried about what you might see?
PAUL: No, I don't think so. It's just that it gets expensive after a while.
MICHAEL: I don't like spending too much time on the computer. It gets stuffy and hot.
SASHA: We're allowed to use the computer as much as we want.
SHANE: But if we want to print something or use the scanner, we have to ask our parents.

Do you spend all day on the computer?
SASHA: No! We do lots and lots of things. We do swimming, we do speed-rollerblading, we do piano, we do tennis.
SHANE: Sometimes we watch television. But mostly, we don't.

How do you think computing can help you with your schoolwork?
MICHAEL: If you're doing programming, it can help you with your Maths. If you're doing graphics, it can improve your imagination.
SHANE: Playing different games where you have to answer questions can help you with the questions you're asked at school.
SASHA: At one stage in school, we were studying bugs, and we had *Microsoft Bugs* on our computer, so we knew a lot of the answers.
KEVIN: Computers don't know everything.
PAUL: I find that programming in Visual Basic helps me with my logic and thinking. If you make one mistake in your programming and it doesn't work, you have to go right back and start again. It teaches you the importance of syntax.
SHANE: You can also go into spellcheck if you make a mistake, and learn how to spell the word right next time.
PAUL: The Internet can help you a lot. I had to do this speech for my school project, so I chose skydiving and just got all the information from the Net.

Do your teachers approve?
PAUL: Not always. Sometimes you'll get given a project, and you'll be told you're not allowed to use the computer.
SASHA: Normally, when our teachers don't say anything about it, we'll use the computer. But our headmaster doesn't really like it. We know this boy, he did this project, and the teacher gave his mother an A plus for it.
KEVIN: You don't even need to ask your mother. You just ask the computer. Go to *Microsoft Encarta*, look something up, select, copy, paste it in.
SHANE: Most of our teachers don't know the programs we use, but they can easily see if you've copied things.
SASHA: Because they'll see all these big words, and ask you to explain, and you'll have to say, 'Oops, I don't know where those came from.'

Do you use the Internet a lot for your homework?
SHANE: We've got the Internet, but we haven't got logged on yet. My dad never wants to plug in the plug.
SASHA: We don't use the computer much for homework. It's only if we want to find out something and even our mom doesn't know the answer, then we'll look it up on the computer.
MICHAEL: My friend, for a science project, wanted me to look up something on incubators. I thought there would be one page on the Internet, but there were 40 million! I'm doing my science project on NASA, so I went to nasa.gov. You can listen to actual space missions. I e-mailed them three weeks ago, but they still haven't answered.
KEVIN: I use the Internet for chatting to people. You type messages, and other people type back.

What kind of people do you chat to?
KEVIN: Everyone.

Do you come across any weird people?
KEVIN: No, not really. Although last night, this big message appears on the screen: 'I am a lesbian.'

So what did you do?
KEVIN: I just typed back, 'Good for you!'

SHANE: The thing that bothers me about the Internet is that everybody in the world can see what you're typing. So you never get to type anything secret.
KEVIN: You could go on to a private channel.
MICHAEL: Or just send e-mail instead of using chat.
SASHA: The other day, at K-Net, we chatted to this girl from Beijing. I asked her if she liked shark-fin soup. She said, 'No, I prefer rice.'
SHANE: We told her we have pizza and cheeseburgers. She hardly ever has that.
SASHA: Once we went into this program where you can look at things in the human body. We saw this virus that looks like a pizza, and we said to our teacher, 'Look, it's just like the pizza we had last night!' She was just, like, 'yuk'.
SHANE: And there was also this other virus that looked like a pancake as well.

Do you use computers a lot at school?
PAUL: We've got computers, but they're just for show. They're ancient 286s. For four years, all we've been doing on them is word processing in DOS. The teacher doesn't even teach us. She just gives us the manual.
KEVIN: Hmmm … we've also got antiques. We only use them for Maths, and so far this year, we haven't used them at all. It's pointless.
MICHAEL: We've got 36 computers in our computer lab, and everyone in the school has their own e-mail address. We use the computers mainly for typing.
SASHA: We've got about 16 computers at our school. They've just moved up from ancient ones to Pentiums. We do all sorts of things when it's our turn. Sometimes we play, sometimes we type, sometimes we make things.
SHANE: We have this game at school called *Typing Attack*. All these words appear on the screen, and you have to type, and little jets shoot at the words. If the jets hit the city, then it's game over.
PAUL: I'm writing a game like that in Visual Basic: A letter appears on the screen, and if you type it, it goes away and you get a point. It's a Windows game, not very advanced. But it's a game you could sell.
KEVIN: I'd like to write games. Real games.

Do your parents or teachers ever ask you for advice on computers?
MICHAEL: Always.
SASHA: Our mom doesn't know a single thing about them!
PAUL: Anyone can teach a teacher about computers. We've got this one computer teacher who says she can make her own screensaver in Windows. But all she actually does is change the writing on the marquee that goes across the screen!
KEVIN: I think teachers are worried that computers are going to take over their jobs.
MICHAEL: It's the way of the future.

Apart from games, what are your favourite programs?
SHANE: CorelDRAW 6.
SASHA: CorelDRAW 7.
SHANE: Well, we had CorelDRAW 6, and then we sold it and bought CorelDRAW 7.
SASHA: I also like Microsoft PowerPoint a lot. You can press a star or circle, and then you can draw a bicycle and make it move.
SHANE: We get new programs about once a month. We got this encyclopaedia, starts with a B…

Britannica?
SASHA: Yes! You could see it was a pirate copy. It didn't have a single picture in it. Just a whole lot of words that somebody had copied.
MICHAEL: For typing, I use Microsoft Word. For Graphics, CorelDRAW and Corel Photo-Paint. Say I want to do a background for a school project. I can import a picture of a dolphin or whatever, and morph the dolphin into the background.
KEVIN: I use this cool graphics program my dad got me from overseas — TrueSpace. It's a 3-D graphics program. I'm still messing around with it, learning all the buttons. You can make animations, but it takes about half an hour to render a 50-frame scene. You walk away, read a book, come back. I'm using it to design a logo for my cousin's Web page.
PAUL: My favourite program right now is Visual Basic. You can do just about anything with it.

These are all very sophisticated programs designed for advanced users. What do you think of programs designed for kids?
KEVIN: Not a lot.
SHANE: Most of them are junk. But some are okay.

What would you like to do when you leave school?
SASHA: I want to be a computer programmer.
SHANE: I'd like to be a computer mentor, teaching kids how to use computers.
PAUL: I don't know what I'm going to do, but I know it's going to involve computers.
KEVIN: You can use computers for any career.
MICHAEL: I want to work for Microsoft.
KEVIN: I wouldn't mind being Bill Gates. Big piggy-bank!

If you could design a dream computer for yourself, what would it do?
PAUL: My dream computer would be one that never runs out of RAM.
SASHA: Mine would probably be one where you can create anything you want, like a robot, and it would just come out of the computer.
SHANE: I wish computers wouldn't take so long to start up. Ours takes about five minutes. I'd also like a computer where you don't ever have to put in a disk. You would just switch it on, and everything you need would be right there.
KEVIN: A computer without Windows 95 would be nice. Boy, does it have a lot of errors.
MICHAEL: I'd like to have a program like they have in the movies to create those, like, whirlwind scenes...
SHANE: Ya! *Twister!* The cow flying across the screen ... ngggy-ooooowww...

(Meeting descends into chaos as the conversation switches to movies and flying animals and speed rollerblading and all sorts of other things only vaguely related to computers.)

Part Two
Software

Chapter 7
So, edutain me!
How to choose and buy children's software

I'm mooching around the software shelves at my local computer hyper, gauging the gore levels of the latest interplanetary shoot-'em-ups, when a familiar face catches my eye. Simba!

The Lion King himself, in the company of his flatulent pal, Pumbaa, and the wisecracking meerkat, Timon. I pick up the box.

It's the CD-ROM of the movie, an 'animated storybook' featuring on-screen narration and a host of games and activities for kids aged three to nine. Forget it. I'm not going to fall victim to yet another Disney merchandising ambush. I put the box back.

Cut to later that night. I've just installed the software — hey, at least it makes a change from the video — and the household's number one Disney addict is sitting in front of the computer screen, eyes wide with anticipation. I start the program.

Nothing happens.

To put it more technical terms, the screen flickers with half-formed animal shapes, accompanied by a strangulated crackle from the stereo speakers. Then everything freezes.

Except for my daughter, who storms off with a petulant command: 'Fix it, Daddy!'

Easier yelled than done. I re-install, read the manual, change the drivers for my video and sound cards. I give up. Finally, I get the *Lion King Animated Storybook* up and roaring on a different computer. And that's when the bugs really begin to work their way to the surface.

Far from being a magical marvel of interactive edutainment, the animated storybook typifies what's wrong with a lot of children's multimedia software. It takes an over-familiar formula, and transfers it to another medium without adding anything but a few hundred rand to the price-tag.

The story is trimmed down, expurgated and accompanied by highlighted text, in the spurious belief that this will develop reading skills. Instead, it develops sitting-there-and-staring-at-the-computer skills. Sure, your kid can click the mouse and 'make the story happen'. But what happens?

A click on Mufasa produces a roar. A click on an elephant produces a trumpet. A click on the sky, and birds fly across it. As Timon might say: 'Biiiiiiig deal.' The 'fun activities' turn out to be equally uninspired and unrewarding, despite the efforts of a syrupy narrator to lend them an air of accomplishment.

And the biggest sin of all for a Disney tie-in: The animation is flat, insipid, and keeps breaking up, even on a powerful Pentium. But so what? Isn't this supposed to be a simple amusement for toddlers? Perhaps. But toddlers don't buy software.

There are so many better ways to keep children amused, and so many worthwhile, witty, original and imaginative software titles out there, that it pays to have a working understanding of what to avoid. But first, two elementary pieces of advice:

➡ When buying children's software, try to buy software that works.
➡ When installing and setting up children's software, make sure children are otherwise occupied.

It's an inviolable law of family computing that something will always go maddeningly wrong when you're trying to set up a program in the presence of an excited, impatient kid. But before you even get that far, there are several other considerations you might want to bear in mind.

Do your homework

Dozens of new children's software titles hit the shelves every year, their slim cargo encapsulated in enough paper, cardboard and shrinkwrap to fill the Grand Canyon.

Extravagant packaging is one of the software industry's biggest irritations, but hold on to that garbage; you're going to need it if the program proves to be faulty or unsuitable. Of course, it's best to buy the right program to begin with, rather than spend hours arguing consumer rights with a computer salesperson afterwards.

So do your homework: Learn to distinguish the good children's titles from the indifferent, the appropriate from the inappropriate, and the truly useful from the merely flashy. At R200 and upwards a throw, children's software shouldn't be an impulse buy. (You're talking to someone who's learned the hard way.)

So how do you arm yourself with the inside information required to make the right choice for your child? Easy. Ask the experts. Other parents of computer-age kids will probably be your most reliable source for unbiased software suggestions.

They rarely have vested interests, they usually live in the real world — or at least, that's where they spend their money — and they'll generally be only too happy to share the benefits of their software-buying-and-trying experience.

If your own circle doesn't extend far enough, and you have access to the Internet, be sure to subscribe to the misc.kids.computer newsgroup on Usenet.

This is a friendly, informal forum for parents from around the world, and the simplest question — 'Can anyone recommend a good drawing and painting program for a three-year-old?' — is guaranteed to elicit a barrage of helpful responses.

You can always back up or balance these parent-in-the-street perspectives by scanning the review sections of a wide range of consumer-oriented PC publications, many with searchable home pages on the Internet. Still, there's no substitute for the hands-on test.

Borrowing from the American model of consumer-friendliness, some South African computer retailers now allow parents and kids to try programs before purchase.

A brightly coloured area will be set aside from the main bustle of the store, and a gallery of computers at kids' eye-level, will be loaded with the latest multimedia software. Somewhere in the background, almost subliminally, the latest Disney video will be playing on television.

You may not be able to test-drive every program in the shop, but at least you'll get a fairly good idea of where to spend your money.

Hunt for the hidden bargains

Every informed consumer knows that it pays to shop around. But when you're buying computer software, you can sometimes save a bundle by shopping around in the same store. Here's an example.

A store of my acquaintance sells the *Grolier Multimedia Encyclopaedia*, an ideal children's resource, for just under R350. Yet, just a few metres away from that price-tag, you can buy the very same CD-ROM for the equivalent of R35. How so?

Because software companies market their goods in strange and mysterious ways. They sell the full retail package at the full retail price, and then they license the software to outside companies for 'bundling' with appropriate hardware, typically a multimedia upgrade kit.

Some of this bundled software then finds its way back on to the shelves, complete with 'Not to be sold separately' warnings that everyone seems happy to ignore. You don't get the wrapping, you don't get the hype, but you do get the goods at a fraction of the price.

Likewise, scrounge around for those bargain-basement '10-CD packs' that round up the best and the worst of multimedia software, at an average of R20 per CD. In amongst the cheap 'n nasty stuff — outdated atlases, low-tech games, leftover clip-art collections — you'll find full versions of some of the best children's software around.

Everything from *Lenny's Toons* to *Putt Putt's Adventures* to *Mavis Beacon's Typing Tutor*. Why pay retail?

Read the small print

Discover a new dimension in storytelling! Experience the magic of Interactive Adventure! Take an incredible journey into a new world of fun and learning!

Now you know why children's software comes in such big packages. They have to make room for the Hollywood-style razzmatazz, the parental ratings, the star-studded seals of independent editorial approval. But you don't have to bother with all that stuff.

What should concern you, as you block up the aisle and mull over your decision, is the teeny print at the bottom of the box (or the side, or the top). The minimum technical requirements.

Here's where you learn the terrible truth: whether your home computer has the processing power, memory, hard drive space, operating system and multimedia capabilities to take you and your family on that incredible journey. Before you splash out, some basic points to ponder.

Is the software on CD-ROM or 3.5-inch disk? Most multimedia titles are CD only, while others offer a choice of both formats. If you've got the hardware, always take the CD. Not only are they blissfully easier to install, but they tend to come with added options and dazzling multimedia tutorials.

Is it the PC or Apple Macintosh version? Good question. If you try to run Mac software on your PC, it probably won't implode, but you will be left with a profound feeling of emptiness and disappointment. Some titles obligingly run on both platforms, in which case the small print will say MAC/MPC or MAC/WINDOWS. Most sensible dealers avoid confusion by assigning Mac titles to their own minority homeland on the shelves.

Will the software run on Windows 3.1, or is it specifically designed for Windows 95? If it says the former, and you're running the latter, don't panic; Windows 95 is designed to be 'backward-compatible' with its predecessor. Windows 95-specific programs, though, are a cunning ploy to force the world's last remaining stragglers to upgrade.

If you're a novice in the minimum technical department, it's a good idea to acquaint yourself with your computer's vital statistics before venturing into the store. Just ask your computer. Entering MSD at the DOS prompt will open a program called Microsoft Diagnostics, and you can print out the necessary information at the click of a mouse.

English English or American English?

We say autumn, they say fall. They say faucet, we say tap. We say boot, they say trunk.

As former colonies divided by a common language, South Africa and America have evolved their own understanding of what constitutes correct English usage.

But while our education system follows the British model, we're forced to be American subjects when it comes to computing. We say program, not programme; disk, not disc; and if you ask a dealer for a 43.18-centimetre monitor, you're more likely to get a blank stare than the regulation 17-inch.

Children's software is similarly dominated by Americanisms: It's all 'math' and 'color' and baseball, from those wonderful people who brought you 'edutainment'. Is there any hope for the Queen's English? A little.

Some of the bigger software publishers now produce Anglocentric versions of their top titles, with the 'proper' pronunciation, spelling and cultural perspective.

The popular *Microsoft Encarta* encyclopaedia is available in a 'World English' edition, complete with video clips of cricket and the Queen, while kids' titles, such as the excellent *3D Movie Maker*, feature Microsoft mascot McZee as a broadly accented Scot rather than a brash American homeboy.

If you prefer the real English thing, without any regional accents to confuse the issue, Dorling Kindersley's superb range of children's multimedia titles are your best bet. And the real South African thing? Forget it.

The market is too small to take our eclectic range of cultures and official languages into account, and South African software developers have been slow in coming up with the right mix of edutainment and local relevance. Just as well we all speak American anyway.

Growing into software

To make it easier for indecisive parents to part with their money, software publishers grade their products according to the age of the intended consumer. Typical age groupings are 2 to 5, 3 to 7, 7 to 9, and 9 to 14.

For the most part, these recommendations are based on the degree of reading, comprehension, reasoning and computing skills required to get the most out of the software. But it's worth remembering that they're recommendations — not restrictions.

The best children's software, like the best children's literature, is ageless and timeless in its appeal. Even the relentless march of technology will not leave it behind. Look at a classic like *Just Grandma and Me*, one of the earliest children's interactive titles.

A three-month-old baby will be captivated by the program's charming animation and sound effects. In toddlerhood, the same child will develop the mouse-skills to explore and interact with the program's deeper layers.

At school-going age, the child will enjoy reading the story by following the highlighted text on-screen. Later, thanks to the miracle of multilingual multimedia, the child will be able to rediscover the story in Japanese or Spanish.

All on one CD, officially aimed at three- to seven-year-olds. Look for software that will grow with your child.

Some of the concepts and subtleties may not mean much to early starters, but there'll always be a picture, sound or action to stimulate curiosity and draw the child back to the program as the years go by.

Putting it to the test
All right: the shrinkwrap's off, the disk's in the drive, eager hands are hovering over keyboard or mouse.

It's time to see whether your disposable income has been wisely disposed of, or whether you're about to enter into a major dispute over that 'We cannot accept returns on opened software' sign at your neighbourhood computer hyper. So how do you judge the lasting value of a piece of multimedia software?

The expression on your child's face may not tell the whole story: Some children have a natural talent for looking underwhelmed. (They're the ones who grow up to become journalists.)

The following pointers may come in handy:

EASE OF NAVIGATION
Starting a kids' program will generally lead you into an opening logo, with an explanatory sequence hosted by a cute cartoon character or hip young role-model.

These sequences are fun and helpful the first few times, but there should be a way of bypassing them as your child becomes familiar with the software. Otherwise, they become a major irritation and source of fidgeting.

The interface should be easy to navigate, with choices clearly labelled or pictured, and written or spoken help close to hand. Response to keyboard or mouse input should be instantaneous, or as close to it as possible. In the age of instant gratification, few kids will have the patience to sit there staring at a 'busy' cursor, even if the cursor is shaped like a frog or a teddy bear.

Double-clicking with a mouse is difficult for many children (and some adults) so the program should respond to commands issued with a single click.

From any point in the program, your child should be able to pause or exit, return to the starting-point, and move on to other activities with ease. Even non-readers should be able to figure their way around. Programs aimed at very young children often bar such exploration, on the grounds that random keyboard or mouse-bashing will lead to chaos.

Even then, there should be a way for parents to control the program. Few things are more infuriating than software that behaves like a runaway train.

Depth of exploration

When you've just spent up to R500 on a children's software title, you don't want it to be tossed aside after one cursory session. You want it to be dynamic, stimulating and multi-dimensional, with a strong element of 'surprise me' at its core.

Children should be able to explore the program in several different ways, and at several different levels of difficulty. The interactive sequences — 'Let's click here and see what happens' — should be witty, wacky or awesome enough to justify the effort and to keep kids coming back for more.

If game-play and problem-solving are involved, there should be constant feedback: applause, encouragement and patient invitations to try again. Many programs, such as the Jumpstart series of learning adventures, will allow you to print out colourful progress reports or certificates suitable for framing.

That's why children like computers. They don't yell at you when you get things wrong, and they shower you with praise when you get things right.

Multimedia or multimediocre?

Wow! Will you take a look at that? An actual video playing in a little window on the computer screen! And listen to this: real hi-fi stereo sound! Now watch what happens when I click on this glowing green icon here…

No doubt about it. Parents and other grown-ups are knocked out by the power of multimedia. But to kids, it's no big deal. Bathed in the blue light of television since birth, they expect nothing less than sound, light and action from any household object with a screen.

Be wary, therefore, of programs that make a big noise about their multimedia content. You may be tempted to choose one CD-ROM encyclopaedia over another because it boasts more video clips, sound clips and 'dazzling animations', but in practice such attractions are often a letdown.

Look for programs that use multimedia not as an end in itself, but as a way of enhancing learning, encouraging interaction and stimulating the imagination. Otherwise, your kid may as well go back to watching television.

Avoid gimmicks
I once bought my daughter a cheerfully decorated toothbrush mug, a matching toothbrush and a small floppy doll with hat. Total cost of items: R299,99.

Okay, I know it sounds extravagant, but somewhere in the packaging was a CD-ROM that promised 'hours of multimedia magic, interactive learning and creative play for your child'. How could I refuse my daughter this?

Well, I could have read the small print and noted that half of the program is in French. Now, as I wait for my daughter to show even the slightest signs of becoming a Francophile, the disc lies discarded and the doll fights a losing battle for attention with Barbie and co.

Moral: Beware of software bearing gifts. Good software is a gift in itself.

Don't underestimate your kid's capabilities
When setting out to buy software for kids, don't limit your shopping to the kids' software shelves. Many computer-savvy kids display a remarkable propensity for outgrowing software deemed appropriate for their age group.

Once they've moved beyond the hand-holding stage, they'll often be quite capable of mastering a software package that doesn't feature feedback from a talking teddy bear.

You'll have to consult with your kid on this matter but, in principle, don't hesitate to choose *Microsoft Encarta* over *Children's Multimedia Encyclopaedia*, *Corel PrintHouse* over *Storybook Weaver*, or, if you've really got a whizzkid on your hands, *TurboCAD* over *Kid CAD*.

Give your kid every opportunity to surprise you, by exploring and mastering software designed for the real world. In the long run, you'll save money too.

21 software packages no family should be without
In no particular order, some personal recommendations...

1. *Just Grandma and Me* **(Living Books)** Little Critter spends a day at the beach with his *gogo*. A multimedia classic, packed with delightful animation and hip references for grown-ups.

2. *My First Incredible, Amazing Dictionary* (Dorling Kindersley) A is for Apple, B is for Book, C is for CD-ROM ... and they don't come much more incredible or amazing than this.

3. *Learning in Toyland* (Fisher-Price) The fun thing about Fisher-Price programs, aside from everything else, is that they're based on Fisher-Price toys. Talk about a dilemma for kids who have them both.

4. *Dr Seuss's ABC* (Living Books) Everyone's favourite family doctor fills impressionable minds with priceless nonsense, on a laugh-and-learn adventure that will have apprentice readers wishing there were more than 26 letters in the alphabet.

5. *The Way Things Work* (Dorling Kindersley) How does a computer compute? How does a hovercraft hover? How does a dishwasher wash dishes? The answers are all here, in charming, witty detail, on this much-acclaimed multimedia version of David Macaulay's international mega-selling book.

6. *Microsoft Encarta* (Microsoft) The MTV of multimedia encyclopaedias. Jazzy, snazzy, alive with visual and verbal information, Encarta educates and entertains like no printed set of shelfbound paperweights could ever hope to do.

7. *A.D.A.M., The Inside Story* (A.D.A.M. Software) Human anatomy stripped bare with wit and multimedia dazzle. If the 'bare' bit worries you, relax: There's a fig-leaf option for sensitive parents.

8. *JumpStart Toddlers* (Knowledge Adventure) First in a series that covers ages one-and-a-half to seven, this superb CD features a range of learning activities that will engage your toddler for hours, as soon as you've had your turn.

9. *Eyewitness Encyclopaedia of Science* (Dorling Kindersley) For a subject that encompasses everything from the Big Bang to a bolt of lightning to the momentum of a rollercoaster, science has suffered greatly from bone-dry teaching methods and a general aura of inaccessibility. Until now.

10. *3D Movie Maker* (**Microsoft**) Cool! Imagine what Spielberg could have done if he'd had this as a kid. Actually, he'd probably still be sitting in front of his computer, making stunning 3-D movies with dazzling visual effects and rude noises in the background.

11. *Math Blaster: In Search of Spot* (**Davidson & Associates**) Spot is lost in space, and it's up to you to find him by solving a series of progressively more difficult mathematical equations in video-arcade style. A total blast. If I'd had this in school, I might have earned an F rather than a G for Maths.

12. *Kid Pix Studio* (**Broderbund**) Almost as much fun as fingerpainting on the dining-room wall, this endlessly entertaining program is guaranteed to unleash the artist in any kid or grown-up.

13. *Kai's Power Goo* (**MetaTools**) You take a picture of a person, animal or object, and you twist it, twirl it, warp it, stretch it, squeeze it, shrink it and otherwise goo it all up until you're rolling hysterically on the floor. If there is a practical use for this program, I hope they never find it.

14. *Where in the World is Carmen Sandiego?* (**Broderbund**) She could be on the Volga. She could be in the Outback. She could be in Paris or Peru or Johannesburg. Track her down, have fun and learn a little about geography in the process.

15. *The Ultimate Human Body* (**Dorling Kindersley**) From the cavernous sweat pores on the surface of your skin, to the moon-like pits and craters of your cartilage, take a good look at yourself on this fantastic voyage through the human machine.

16. *Microsoft Dinosaurs* (**Microsoft**) The T-Rex of dinosaur primers, combining depth of knowledge with slick interactive design and a monster sense of fun.

17. *Putt-Putt Goes to the Moon* (**Humungous Entertainment**) Talking purple jalopy found on lunar surface, teaching kids to count, recognise words and play logic puzzles. Film at 11.

18. *Kid's Typing* (**Sierra Online**) Hey, kids, you can't compute if you can't type. And if you can't type, Spooky the friendly ghost is just the type of tutor you need.

19. *Chronicle of the 20th Century* (**Dorling Kindersley**) It's not quite over yet, but few will deny that the 20th century has been one of history's most awesome epochs. This CD-ROM has several advantages over the hardback edition, notably the fact that it won't land you in hospital if you drop it on your toe.

20. *Greetings Workshop* (**Microsoft**) Publishing barons, young and old, will enjoy making personalised cards, calendars, posters and other fun items with this easy-to-use program, part of Microsoft's bargain *Home Essentials* suite.

21. *Crayola Art Studio* (**Micrografx**) The most fun a kid can have without a pack of Crayola. Hey, look at this! The program includes a free pack of Crayola! Hmmm. Love that smell.

Chapter 8

Try before you buy — the shareware concept

How to get great children's software for next to nothing

It may be fun, colourful, exciting, educational and entertaining, but there's one thing children's software generally isn't: cheap.

As those credit card bills pile up, and your multimedia wonderchild studiously ignores her latest R599 CD-ROM in favour of an old Winnie the Pooh jigsaw puzzle, you may be pleased to learn that there's a more cost-effective way of building up a library of useful programs. It's called 'shareware'.

Shareware is software for free, but it isn't free software. (Unless, of course, it's freeware. *See overleaf* for explanation.) You can download shareware in vast quantities from the Internet, copy and distribute it to your heart's content, and try it out for between 15 and 90 days.

After that, if the program meets your needs, you're expected to pay up under what is quaintly known as the 'honour system'. In return, you'll be e-mailed a password or code which will allow you to continue using the program and access its full range of features.

You may also be entitled to a printed manual, free upgrades and online technical support. And what if you don't like the program? Simple. You erase it from your hard drive and get on with your life.

This principle of 'try before you buy' has become firmly entrenched in the software industry, to the extent that many major manufacturers now offer downloadable trial versions of their megabuck commercial packages.

Since shareware authors usually have negligible overheads and marketing costs, they can afford to sell their software for next to nothing. But don't be fooled by the price-tag.

The best shareware is as good as, and sometimes better than, the best commercial software you'll find on the shelves. All that's missing is the shrinkwrap, the fancy packaging and the famous brand name.

Coming up: a guide to some of the best children's shareware on the market, and where to find it. But first, some explanations:

Shareware Fully-functional computer software distributed outside mainstream retail channels on a try-before-you-buy basis. Numerous shareware programs are designed to stop working at the end of the trial period, while others will allow you to carry on regardless.

Freeware Like the name says. Freeware authors are usually amateur developers or lobbyists, who are only too happy to have their programs tried and tested by as wide a range of users as possible. Even so, few of them will complain too loudly if you choose to send a small donation out of gratitude.

Careware As above, with one small proviso: If you like the program, you're expected to go out and do something caring for the environment or your fellow humans. If only more products were distributed in this manner.

Nagware Shareware that persists in reminding you, through intrusive 'pop-up' screens and other sneaky methods, that you're using a shareware program and it would be nice if you decided to pay for it.

Crippleware Shareware that defeats the purpose of shareware by blocking some of its most vital functions until you cough up. Avoid. Your software shouldn't be allowed to hold you to ransom.

Postcardware Author expects nothing in return for the program, but would appreciate a scenic postcard from your home town. Too bad if you happen to live in Welkom.

Demoware Demonstration versions of commercial software packages. Usually, these demos are little more than glorified adverts, but there are notable exceptions (as we'll soon find out).

Where to find shareware

You'll occasionally find children's shareware, in stiffy disk or CD-ROM format, attached to slim but pricy overseas computer magazines that you might otherwise have no interest in buying.

Resist the temptation, and rather head straight for the world's largest treasure-trove of virtually free stuff. The Internet. (If you're still looking for a good reason to get connected, you've just found it.) Shareware sites abound on the World Wide Web, the people-friendly area of the Net where you and your kids are most likely to hang out.

Start your journey at one of the following all-purpose repositories, where a search on 'children' will turn up masses of shareware for DOS, Windows 3.1 and Windows 95:

Rocket Download
WWW address: http://www.rocketdownload.com
The rockingest shareware site on the Web, with eye-popping graphics and a wide range of cool stuff for kids.

Shareware.com
WWW address: http://www.shareware.com
A mind-bogglingly big site, updated daily.

WinSite Archive
WWW address: http://www.winsite.com
Probably your best bet if you're still running Windows 3.1.

ZDNet Software Library
WWW address: http://www.hotfiles.com/index.html
Run by America's most prominent publisher of computer magazines, this well-designed site features a generous selection of reviewed and rated programs under 'Home & Education'.

These sites specialise in children's shareware:

Lawrence Goetz's Home Page
WWW address: http://pages.prodigy.com/VDJW65A/
From Larry's *Master the Mouse* to *Wacky Tic-Tac-Toe*, excellent educational programs from one of the most prolific shareware authors.

Math Shareware and Freeware
WWW address:
http://forum.swarthmore.edu/shareware/shareware.by.topic.html
Algebra, geometry, calculus, fractals, trigonometry and all that terrifying stuff, made less so for older scholars.

Tigger's Home
WWW address: http://www.gamesdomain.com/tigger/sw-pc.html [annotated: kidsdomain.com/]
A computer mom's personal choice of close to 200 tried-and-tested shareware programs for toddlers and pre-teens.

How to grab all the shareware you want

Copying a program from the Internet on to your computer is a simple three-click process that will soon become intuitive. Click on the filename to begin downloading, click to save the file to disk, and click again to accept the suggested location on your hard drive. Shareware programs tend to have names like XFV20FN.ZIP, so make a note of the location and filename if you don't want to spend hours sifting through your directories afterwards.

It also pays to check that the file you're about to download is in the right format for your operating system. Remember, you *can* run a Windows 3.1 program under Windows 95, but *not* the other way round. Finally, look at the size of the file, as expressed in kilobytes (Kb) or megabytes (MB).

As a rough guide, a 1MB file will take 10 to 20 minutes to download if you're using a 28.8kps modem. If it seems to be taking forever, click 'cancel' to end the download, and try again when Internet traffic is quieter (early in the morning, South African time).

Most programs on the Internet are distributed in compressed format, usually with a 'zip' file-extension. That means you have to 'unzip' them before you can try them out. The best zipper/unzipper on the market is WinZip, a classic example of a shareware program that is streets ahead of its commercial competition. Get it at
http://www.winzip.com

If your downloaded file has an 'exe' extension, on the other hand, you need only double-click the filename to begin the installation process.

Extremely technical addendum: You can also download many shareware files through a process called 'FTP' or 'File Transfer Protocol'. This is often quicker and smoother than downloading from a Web site, but you'll need an extra piece of software called an 'FTP client'. Try CuteFTP, a user-friendly little program that tries very hard to make the process as painless as possible, available at http://www.cuteftp.com

A suggested library of children's shareware

EARLY LEARNING
Amy's Fun-2-3 Adventure (DOS)
WWW address: http://www.devasoft.com/home.htm
Independent tests prove that kids as young as 18 months adore Amy, a spiky-haired canine with a talent for teaching the rudiments of reading and counting.

Baby Keys (DOS)
WWW address:
http://www.rocketdownload.com/details/kids/bbkey.htm
Quick! Come see baby using the computer! Well, actually, just bashing the keys, and the computer is making noise, music and pretty pictures as reward. Proof that you're never too young to have fun on a computer.

Farnsworth Ferret's Fun Pack (Windows 95)
WWW address: http://www.elpin.com
Kid Match, Kid Scramble, Math Invaders, Copy Cat and Kid Paint. Five fun games from the user-friendliest ferret in Computerland.

SUMS AND NUMBERS
CatMinus for Windows (Windows 3.1/95)
WWW address: http://www.shareware.com
A game of cat and mouse with as many minusses and plusses. Then again, it is designed to teach pre-schoolers and early learners the basics of addition and subtraction.

Millie's Math House (Windows 95)
WWW address: http://www.indelibleink.com/kded040.html
Bugs, mice, jellybeans and cookies are just some of the attractions of this award-winning activity centre, which focuses on shapes, patterns and maths the silly Millie way.

Roxie's Math Fish (Windows 3.1/95)
WWW address: http://members.aol.com/latticewrk/lattice.htm
A colourful and noisy game of 'Go Fish', with a cat called Roxie as gamesmaster, and mathematical equations in place of the fish.

Words and letters
Bobby's First Letters (Windows 3.1/95)
WWW address: http://www.shareware.com
B is for Bobby, who deserves an A for this simple but effective introduction to the alphabet.

Show and Tell (Windows 3.1/95)
WWW address: http://www.shareware.com
Elementary reading made fun and easy through spoken words and charming pictures.

Ultimate Language Tutor (Windows 95)
WWW address: http://softsite.com/ulti/4langd.htm
Explore the basics of four European languages through flashcard drills and quizzes.

Weekly Speller (Windows 3.1/95)
WWW address: http://www.datacom.ca/~ron/
A colourful and easy-to-use tuition tool for kids who spell weakly.

Word Wrestle (Windows 95)
WWW address: http://www.smartcode.com
Get to grips with the mysteries of the English language on this puzzling but very wordy addition to the family software shelf.

Arts and crafts
Child's Play II (Windows 3.1/95)
WWW address: http://www.siteit.com/asl
Painting made fun, with music, noises and voices adding extra dimensions to an artful example of excellence in children's shareware.

Lil' Picasso (Windows 3.1/95)
WWW address: http://www.pc-shareware.com/

Picasso tried to paint like a child. Now your child can try to paint like Picasso would have painted if he'd known how to handle a mouse.

Maths, science and other scary stuff
BlackBox Math Expert (Windows 95)
WWW address: http://www.compuserve.com.au/sci_math/index.htm
A highly acclaimed Australian program designed to make high school algebra less painful than it sounds.

Graphmatic (Windows 95)
WWW address: http://www.shareware.com
Widely acclaimed for helping students plot trigonometry and calculus equations with power and precision.

Microscope (DOS)
WWW address:
http://www.microscopy-uk.org.uk/prodir/software/softmol.html
An eye-boggling microbiology package from the UK designed to give students an insight into the world as seen through a powerful laboratory microscope. A huge and complicated download, but well worth the hassle.

MineraLogic (Windows 3.1)
WWW address: http://www.zdnet.com
A logical, systematic, easy-to-navigate database of 70 common minerals. So they say.

Life's little lessons
Animated Clock (Windows 95)
WWW address: http://www.eden.com/~flixprod/
It's never too early to teach your kids to tell the time, especially when the timepiece is a clock with a cuckoo sense of humour.

Interactive Dental Office (DOS)
WWW address: http://www.catalog.com
If getting your kids to go to the dentist for their regular ch like pulling teeth, make a game of it with this informative taining dental strategy challenge.

Games and hobbies
CyberSky (Windows 3.1/95)
WWW address: http://www.astro.ucla.edu
An out-of-this-world astronomy program that will have young and not-so-young minds reaching for the sky.

Greatest Paper Airplanes (Windows 3.1/95)
WWW address: http://www.khs.com
A soaring multimedia introduction to the history and principles of flight, complete with instructions for a squadron of origami planes.

Snakes (Windows 95)
WWW address: http://www.ozemail.com.au/~dbscon/
Not to mention Ladders. This is the classic boardgame, with colourful graphics, fun sound effects and built-in counting lessons.

Commercial demos
So infectious is the spirit of shareware on the Internet, that even the mighty mega-corporations are muscling in on the act. Take advantage of their generosity by downloading demonstration versions that range from barely playable to fully functional. Sure, you'll spend hours online, but it's a lot easier (and cheaper) than trying to get your money back from the software salesman.

Castle Infinity
WWW address: http://www.castleinfinity.com
Limited-function demo of the wacky multi-player game for switched-on cyberkids. Pentium and Windows 95 required.

O'Connor House Software
WWW address: http://www.kingfoo.com
Demos of the interactive early learning programs *Foo Castle*, *Alfoobet* and *123 Foo*.

Edmark
WWW address: http://www.mathclub.com
If you think geometry can never be fun, you're probably right. Your kids might disagree as they get to grips with their free *Electronic Geoboard*.

The Edutainment Company
WWW address: http://www.edutainco.com
From Putt-Putt to Dr Seuss to SimCity, megatons of marvellous demos from several top software publishers. Make this your first stop on the freebie trail.

Gryphon Software
WWW address: http:www.gryphonsw.com
Functional but limited demo of *Gryphon Bricks,* an infinitely absorbing virtual construction kit for kids aged 5 to 105, plus a wide range of other special effects and activity software.

Interplay
WWW address: http://www.interplay.com/games/salemari.html
Can a small Italian plumber with a moustache teach your kids typing? You'd be surprised. *Mario Teaches Typing* is the name of the game.

Microsoft
WWW address: http://www.microsoft.com
Fully functional demos of some superb children's programs, including *Nickelodeon 3D Movie Maker, Magic School Bus* and *Creative Writer.* You'll also find a 60-day trial version of the wonderful *Microsoft Publisher* here, but beware — it's an humungously big download.

PF Magic
WWW address: http://www.pfmagic.com
Dogz, Catz and Oddballz are the cutesy virtual petz that have taken kidz and adultz by storm. Get your free demos here.

Sierra Online
WWW address: http://www.sierra.com/archive/demos
Playable demos of *3-D Ultra Pinball, The Incredible Machine, Cyber-Gladiators* and several other awesome adventure games.

Soleil Software
WWW address: http://soleil.com
Try out a range of excellent multilingual learning adventures, including *Zurk's Learning Safari, Zurk's Rainforest Lab* and *World Walker.*

Vividus Software
WWW address: http://www.vividus.com
Free 30-day demo of *Web Workshop*, a cool World Wide Web authoring package for kids. Windows 95 only.

Chapter 9

Blam! Splat! Whoomph!
It's only a game

You couldn't hope to meet two nicer kids than Harrison Francis (9) and his brother Carson (7). They're friendly, they're polite, and they almost always remember to pack away their toys.

Although they'll occasionally trade playful punches or karate kicks, there's nothing in their behaviour to suggest that they'd ever dream of harming another human being. But who said anything about human beings?

Upstairs, in the 'Doom Room' of the Francis household in Blairgowrie, Harrison's finger hovers over a row of numbers on his computer keyboard. What's it going to be this time? The rocket launcher? The double-barrelled shotgun? The BFG 9000 plasma rifle? No. This time, it's personal. He chooses the chainsaw. In an instant, Harrison is transformed from nice, quiet boy into tough American Marine, hunting down mutant zombies in a toxic Martian wasteland.

It's quiet in here. Too quiet.

Suddenly, the strangulated growl of something not quite animal, not quite human. Harrison spins around. It's a vision from the depths of hell. A hulking, skinless demon with hot coals for eyes and fangs as sharp as a razor. Quick! The chainsaw!

Harrison grits his teeth and hits Ctrl. Flesh tears, blood spurts, body parts fly to the floor. There's only one sound louder than the screaming of the chainsaw and its victim, and that's Harrison's little brother jumping up and down yelling: 'My turn! My turn!'

Wrong. It's Dad's turn. As Stephen Francis makes his choice — the good old-fashioned Gatling gun, capable of mowing down up to seven zombie mutants at a time — it's clear that computer games have come a long way since the days of *Pong*, *Pac-Man* and *Space Invaders*. Rudimentary graphics and cheap blooping noises have given way to full-motion video, 3-D environments, thumping rock soundtracks and characters that walk, talk, shoot, grunt, kick and kill. Mostly, kill.

The violence may be cartoonish (you can shrink your enemy and squash him with your boot in *Duke Nukem 3D)*, or gross (you can rip out your opponent's spinal column or still-beating heart in *Mortal Kombat)*, or just plain gruesome (you can watch a woman being strapped to a table and force-fed raw meat in *Phantasmagoria)*.

But is there real and lasting harm in any of this? Can computer games turn your kids into antisocial deviants? Can excessive game-playing be injurious to their health? And how do you get to the seventeenth level of *Doom* without being torn from limb to limb or fried in a pool of boiling lava? We'll get on to that in a moment. First, let's take a closer look at some of the issues.

Games and violence

It must be said that there are such things as non-violent computer games with socially redeeming qualities. There is the atmospheric *Myst*, which invites you to solve a mind-boggling mystery on an eerily abandoned island. There is the intriguing *SimCity*, which puts you in charge of designing and managing a bustling metropolis. There are boardgames, simulations and role-playing adventures, which test your powers of strategy and reasoning to the limit. But nothing appeals to the instincts of the average computer game player like a little ultra-violence. (Except maybe a lot of ultraviolence.)

With their high-calibre action, flying body parts and reservoirs of blood, today's computer games are part of a culture that says violence is cool.

BLAM! A man gets his head blown off in a Tarantino movie. SPLAT! A costumed superhero collides with a referee in *Wrestlemania*. WHOOMPH! A pipe bomb turns a mutant to mincemeat in *Duke Nukem 3D*.

Over-the-top and tongue-in-cheek, such violence is not meant to be taken seriously, except perhaps as ironic commentary on violence itself. But the big difference with computer game violence is that you're the one calling the shots. And while a movie may be over in 90 minutes, a game with multiple levels and variations can keep a player occupied for hours at a stretch. As the adrenaline surges and the body count mounts, what are the chances that an impressionable youngster could get the urge to pick up a real weapon and go on a rampage against, um, real mutant zombie aliens?

Fortunately, they're not very high. Although numerous attempts have been made to draw links between simulated violence and the real thing, there's no compelling evidence to suggest that computer games can turn kids into killing machines. On the contrary, a strong case could be made for the benefits of game-playing as an outlet for fantasy and aggression.

Kids have always played war games. They've always been deeply fascinated by tales of blood and gore, as many a parent has been shocked to discover while reading a bedtime story from those masters of gratuitous ultraviolence, the Brothers Grimm. But real violence, the kind you see on the eight o'clock news, has its roots in a complex mix of social, environmental and political factors. You can't blame games or fairy tales or heavy metal music. You can only teach your kids where to draw the line.

As PC parent Stephen Francis puts it: 'I only know that my kids can tell the difference between a game and reality. It's been embedded into their brains that monsters and zombies aren't real. I don't believe they crave the bloodshed in a game like *Doom* — they crave the action and the challenge of trying to find a way out.'

Nevertheless, in our already ultraviolent society, parents have a right to be concerned about unacceptable levels of violence in what are supposed to be forms of amusement. That's where parental guidance comes in.

Just like movies, many of today's popular games are rated according to their degree of violence, sex or nudity, and offensive language. The Recreational Software Advisory Council (RSAC), a voluntary body formed in response to threats of legislation by the American Senate, uses a complex system of alpha-numerical codes to help parents make an informed choice.

The rating for Disney's *101 Dalmations Animated Storybook*, for instance, is V0 SN0 L0. That means no violence, no sex or nudity, and no offensive language.

Pick up *Doom II*, on the other hand, and the sticker will say V3a SN0 L1a, meaning 'blood and gore', no sex or nudity, and 'mild expletives'. Now, if you dare, try the notorious *Phantasmagoria*, which earns a V3a SN3c L3 for its violence, 'non-explicit sexual activity', and 'strong, vulgar language'.

Do these ratings make a difference? Probably not. They're not enforced by law, and retailers are under no obligation to observe them. But at least you won't be able to say you didn't know what your kids were letting themselves in for.

Many games with 'adult content' also allow parents to exercise their guidance more directly by password-protecting certain levels and selecting milder degrees of V, SN and L.

Bear in mind that computer-savvy kids will often find a way around these restrictions. It may even become a part of the game.

The best defence is inside knowledge: Take an active interest in the games your kids and their pals are playing, and draw parameters appropriate to their age. Some games just aren't meant to be played by very young children.

Games and health

Listening to heavy metal music can damage your eardrums. Rollerblading can bruise your knees. Tennis can hurt your elbow. It should come as no surprise, therefore, that an activity as captivating as computer game-playing — or 'gaming' as it's now commonly known — can have physical side-effects of its own.

The most serious and sensational of these is something called 'VGRS' or 'Video Game Related Seizure'. The cause: repetitive, high-intensity flashes of colour or white light, combined with swiftly changing images on a computer screen. The symptoms: blurred vision, eye or muscle twitches, impaired consciousness and episodes of 'intense memory recall and confusion'.

Although dozens of cases have been documented in medical literature since the advent of video games, the condition is believed to affect only those individuals with a known predisposition to epileptic attacks. As a result, many action games now carry epilepsy warnings in those manuals nobody reads. But as Professor Peter Cooper, head of Paediatrics at the University of the Witwatersrand points out, epileptic seizures can be triggered by any pattern of flashing or flickering lights, whether at a disco or on a TV screen or in a car travelling along an avenue of trees in bright sunlight.

Video Game Related Seizure is very uncommon, he says, but the all-absorbing intensity of the gaming experience calls for certain precautions. Children should not sit or stand too close to the screen, and should avoid playing when tired. The computer room should be adequately lit. Persuade your kids to hit the Escape key and take a break from the action every 10 or 15 minutes. Otherwise, stand by to deal with a far more prosaic reaction to excessive game-playing — *nausea*.

With their first-person perspective, gliding motion and in-your-face action, games like *Doom* and *Duke Nukem 3D* are as close as you can get to virtual reality without wearing a silly helmet. But the effects are the same. Your eyes tell your brain that you're moving through a fantastic landscape. Your body tells your brain that you're not. These conflicting signals can induce disorientation and motion sickness, and can serve as instant aversion therapy for some players. But most will simply get up and wander around in a mild daze, secretly relishing the curious sensation that they're still trapped inside a 3-D game. The recommended treatment for someone who has been 'Doomstruck' is a brief lie-down, a fizzy drink and a temporary ceasefire in the war against the aliens.

But don't worry about it too much. Even the most avid game player will get the message when the body sends a signal saying 'enough is enough'. In the meantime, keep a lookout for other potential health problems, such as dry and burning eyes — blink rates tend to slow down dramatically when you're viewing motion on a computer screen — and aching wrists and tendons that could signal the onset of a repetitive strain injury.

If all else fails, buy your kid a pair of rollerblades. And don't forget the protective clothing.

Games and learning

In the same way that you can learn a lot about the principles of physics by taking a ride on a roller-coaster, there's a lot you can learn about the basics of computing by playing a few levels of *Duke Nukem 3D*.

From hand-eye co-ordination to mouse skills to keyboard commands, computer games are an everyday example of education in action. Set in labyrinthine underworlds or the depths of outer space, games can teach children about architectural perspective and astronomy, as well as the effects of high-calibre ammunition on ... okay, let's stop fooling ourselves.

Games are for fun. They're for thrills, spills and the challenge of competition against the machine or your buddies. That's why you won't find *real* games in most computer laboratories or after-school centres. The best a game-crazy kid can hope for is *Math Blaster*, which uses non-violent arcade-style action to teach fractions, equations and geometry, or *Where in the World Is Carmen Sandiego*, which tests your knowledge of geography as you track a gang of baddies across the globe.

Still, the very fact that educational programs can use game-playing as a vehicle for learning suggests that games themselves can have educational benefits that may be purely unintentional.

On the most basic level, games can serve as the gateway to a world of wider possibilities, acquainting young players with the fundamentals of computing, and encouraging an enthusiasm for technology. Even the most apparently mindless shoot-'em-up demands quick thinking and alertness on the part of the player, who must find a way out of the maze without being zapped. Proof of the challenge is that real American marines use *Doom* to sharpen their combat reflexes, which means we can all sleep safer in the event of an alien invasion.

But the real test of brainpower begins further up the scale, with quest and adventure games that require planning, strategy, patience and the ability to think laterally in a tight situation.

Whether these skills can be transferred to the real world is another matter but, at the very least, mastering a fiendishly difficult game (without resorting to the cheat codes) can boost feelings of self-esteem, control and positive achievement. Okay, now it's your turn.

Games and parents

Many parents are quick to dimiss computer games as noisy, mind-wasting activities with no socially redeeming value. The turning-point usually comes when a child looks over his shoulder and asks, 'Want to have a go?'

Games are an integral part of children's computing, and the only way to understand their appeal is to cast aside your preconceptions and become a player. The right game, in the right hands, played with the right frame of mind can absorb, transfix, challenge, energise and frustrate like no other activity on earth. Just ask Gary Kasparov.

As a family activity, gaming can also serve as a rewarding alternative to communal television watching. An American researcher once noted that computer games brought families together for shared recreation 'more than any other activity in recent memory'.

With this in mind, here are some games that will have your family fighting like never before.

3-D Ultra Pinball (**Sierra Online**) Full tilt ahead for a classic arcade game in this lightning-fast epic set in outer space.

Diablo (**Blizzard**) A darkly compelling adventure set in the Dark Ages. Remember: The family that slays together, stays together.

Gabriel Knight II: The Beast Within (**Sierra Online**) Puzzling, haunting, richly cinematic, this edge-of-your-seat adventure is gaming at its finest. Not recommended for whatever you call people who are afraid of werewolves.

Goosebumps: Escape From Horrorland (DreamWorks Interactive) Kids who love the spooky books by R.L. Stine will jump out of their seats with terror and glee as they try to find their way out of the world's scariest theme park.

Kasparov's Gambit (Electronic Arts) Can you beat the man who lost to the machine? The ultimate chess-player's challenge, with gorgeously rendered 3-D pieces and digitised commentary from the master himself.

Microsoft Flight Simulator (Microsoft) What pilots do for fun. With stunning graphics and mind-boggling attention to detail, it's as close as you'll get to the real thing without going to flight school.

Monster Truck Madness (Microsoft) Step into the cab of Bigfoot, the world's most abominable truck, and crush your puny opponents on sand, grass, asphalt or mud. Anything but tar.

Need for Speed (Electronic Arts) The object is not to drive like a lunatic. The object is to beat the other guy who is driving like a lunatic. Breathtaking 3-D action, with thrills and spills you can almost feel.

If you have access to the Internet, be sure to visit Happy Puppy.com at http://www.happypuppy.com

It's the best gaming site on the World Wide Web, with access to tips, hints, cheat codes, walkthroughs and downloadable demos that will help you decide what games are right or wrong for your kids.

Chapter 10

Digital dolls and virtual shopping

Computers are a girl's best friend

Give me a break! Just because some girls don't want to play a game where you go around collecting points for every head you blow off, doesn't mean we want to sit around putting make-up on a Barbie face.

JUNIOR HIGH SCHOOL STUDENT, ALASKA, USA.
FROM *Computers and the Internet: Listening to Girls' Voices*,
A MASTER'S THESIS BY DEE DEE WILCOX

She stands alone in the corner of the computer store, long blonde hair flowing down to impossibly narrow hips. In the midst of monster trucks, kung-fu killers, and flesh-eating zombies from outer space, she smiles serenely, bearing the regal standard of one of the world's most endangered species.

She is Barbie, the Plastic Princess, on CD-ROM.

Search a little harder on the software shelves and you might find others of her kind: Carmen Sandiego, the globe-trotting villainess with the lipstick-red fedora; Sheila Rae, the fearless, feisty field-mouse; and little Madeline, merrily skipping her way to school along a bright Parisian boulevard.

Otherwise, if you're looking for software role models and heroines for young girls, welcome to the harsh truth of kids' computing today: It's a boy's, boy's, boy's, boy's world. Of course, we're not going to make any sexist assumptions about this. There's no reason why a young girl, sitting at her computer, shouldn't be able to race a monster truck over rough terrain or wield a plasma rifle in a post-apocalyptic landscape.

But would she really want to? Or would she rather use her computing skills in a more constructive fashion, designing party outfits and fairytale adventures for the digital version of the doll in her cupboard? Such questions are largely irrelevant in the early years of computer discovery when boys and girls fall equally under the spell of these cool new playthings.

Guided by androgynous, anthropomorphic characters — a gopher named Giggles, a car named Putt-Putt, a little critter named Little Critter — kids compute in a gender-free world where anything is possible. The computer is a toy, an ever-willing facilitator for fun and learning across the Great Divide.

Then, suddenly, somewhere between nine and adolescence, reality hits home with a vengeance. The battle-lines are drawn. Boys become fixated with the power of computers, seeing them not only as weapons of simulated mass destruction, but as ends in themselves. Wow! Look at those graphics! Listen to that sound! Check out that joystick!

Girls, who have better things to do with their lives, abandon interest altogether or narrow their focus to the specifics of what a computer can do. Can it help me keep a secret diary? Can it print out my school project? Can it tell me everything there is to know about Brad Pitt?

Yes, these are generalisations. Yes, they're perceptions. But they're reflected and reinforced by the packages you'll find on the software shelves, so much so that a new revolution is brewing in the trenches.

Spearheaded by a bold new breed of programmers, developers and distributors, girls are fighting back. They're rediscovering the liberating power of technology, and reclaiming their inalienable right to be computer geeks.

Why should guys have all the fun? Why should boys have all the cool toys? Why are there so few really cool software programs for girls? Jackie Swanson (9), crazy about computers and bored out of her mind, was asking all the questions. Her mother, Janese, a software producer and Doctor of Education, was listening. Result: Girl Tech.

Driven by a mission to make technology cool and fun for girls, Swanson's company publishes books and CD-ROMs, runs a buzzing, vibey site on the World Wide Web (http://www.girltech.com), and designs toys and games that promise action and adventure without the threat of ultraviolence. But is there a market for software that appeals only to girls? Just ask Barbie.

Her début CD-ROM, *Barbie Fashion Designer* (Mattel Media), annihilated even the goriest boys-only shoot-'em-ups on the American software sales charts, shattering records for games as well as educational titles. Strictly speaking, it doesn't belong in either category. Aimed at girls aged six and up, it's a simple design-a-dress-for-Barbie activity program, the first in a series of logical tie-ins for an accessory-crazy babe who already boasts her own pink Pentium.

Is it clever merchandising? Is it smart software? Or is it a winner by default in a market dominated by such titles as *CyberGladiators* (smash, bash and thrash your way to victory in combat), *Road Rash* (knock down pedestrians and outrun the cops in suburban motorcycle street-racing) and *Krush Kill 'n' Destroy* (er, crush, kill and destroy everything in your path)?

Either way, Barbie is not the first software superstar with a feminine twist. In the mid-Eighties, sassy Carmen Sandiego, leader of a gang of international no-gooders called V.I.L.E., dared amateur sleuths to track her down in exotic locations, sneakily leaving a trail of educational clues about geography and foreign cultures. Carmen is still going strong, thanks in part to her proven ability to appeal to boys as well as girls.

But for new computer companies like Girl Tech, Her Interactive and Girl Games, boys don't even make it on to the agenda — except as passing topics of discussion. Research tells these companies what they've suspected all along: Girls are different from boys. As sociologist Sherry Turkle puts it, there are two styles of computing displayed by younger users. There is the risk-taking style, characterised by 'testing the limits of machine and self through mastery and manipulation of the computer environment'. And there is the relational style, marked by 'an artistic, almost tactile style of identification with computational objects'. Translation: Boys want to rule the world; girls want to relate.

In an experiment conducted at the Massachusetts Institute of Technology (MIT), a group of nine- and ten-year-olds were asked to design a software game to teach younger kids the basics of fractions. Across the Great Divide, the boys in the group designed action-packed adventure games, with heinous punishments awaiting players who got the answers even fractionally wrong. On-screen figures would be 'kicked to the moon', 'turned into an ice cube' or 'sent frying to the underworld', and the game would come to an abrupt end.

The girls in the group adopted a more humanitarian approach. Theme-based activities took the place of gruelling quests, with players required to ski down a slope, move around a spider web, or land at an airport. In the case of a wrong answer, the most brutal punishment the girls could dream up was this: 'The player has to talk in French.' In the real world, software developers are beginning to take note.

The big lesson is that girls are turned off by mindless, noisy, arcade-style shoot-'em-ups. What they like is logic puzzles and games of strategy, like the simple yet fiendishly absorbing *Tetris*, where the player has to manoeuvre falling geometric shapes into position. What they also like, it seems, is doing what girls around the world have been doing since the beginning of time. Chatting. Talking. Schmoozing. Sharing ideas, opinions and inside information on everything from parents to friends to hairdos to dreams to — gasp! — boys. In *Let's Talk about Me* (Girl Games), pre-teens can design a dream wardrobe, experiment with hairstyles, analyse their horoscopes, keep a daily diary, plan nutritious meals, and 'learn how to cope with this challenging stage in life'. At the same time, without making too much of a big deal about it, they'll be learning how to cope with the challenges of computer technology.

Likewise, *McKenzie & Me* (Her Interactive) is a five CD-ROM package that gives tech girls endless opportunities to interact with Kim, Carly, Elizabeth, Sam, McKee and Trish. Guided by this cool-talking sextet of best buddies, you can mooch at the Virtual Mall, try on over 400 totally awesome outfits, take on a part-time job, peruse a portrait gallery of boys to sigh for, and learn how to apply make-up with expert ease. Indeed, *McKenzie & Me* even comes with a free tube of lipgloss.

But is this what girls really want from computer software? Don't they want role models? Don't they want action heroes? Don't they want Sigourney Weaver in *Alien,* Linda Hamilton in *Terminator,* Sandra Bullock in *The Net?* Don't they even want Pac-Girl?

Not really. What they want is well-designed software that recognises and acknowledges 'female styles of conceptualisation and interaction', according to a landmark study sponsored by the Centre for Research on Parallel Computation in the USA. Thirty girls, aged between 12 and 17, with varying degrees of computer interest and ability, took part in a three-day exploration and discussion workshop.

They played games, browsed the Internet, swapped ideas, and composed wish-lists based on 'what you would like technology to do in your wildest dreams'. Some of the findings: Girls prefer random exploration and free-form play to structured competition. They're interested in open-ended activities, rather than games that require the player to rack up points and complete one increasingly difficult level before moving on to the next. Girls want atmosphere and texture in a computer gaming environment. They want good, memorable music and recognisably human voices, not the robotic drones commonly heard in sci-fi action games. Girls enjoy the opportunity to solve challenging puzzles and problems in their own time. They don't necessarily view 'winning the game' as an essential objective, and they're frustrated by games that 'kill' you if you make a wrong move. Girls want intuitive, easy-to-use software that explains and reveals itself as you go along. They will only refer to the manual as a last resort. (In this respect, they're not that different from boys.) Girls would like computers and software to enhance their experience of the world, from the familiar to the fantastic. They'd like to bungee-jump by computer, meet their dream dates, try on an endless variety of clothes, hop from career to career, host an Oprah-style talkshow on teen topics, and travel the world without their parents.

These preferences and ideas are already beginning to filter their way into software design, but the greater challenge is to convince girls (and their parents) that computing isn't merely a male prerogative. What the world needs is a 'Jill Gates': a powerful, influential, universally known computer pioneer and visionary who just happens to be a woman.

Of course, there's no shortage of high-profile women in the computer industry. Well, actually, there is. Shannah Albert, a computer consultant and trainer for the Price Waterhouse group, worries that 'the world is missing out on great computer scientists' because so many women never discover their talents in this area.

In high school, Shannah was the only girl in her advanced Computer Science class; later, as a Computer Science teacher, she was still the only female in class. The computer laboratory was over-run by boys, exploring, 'tinkering', creating their own projects or programs. The few girls who used the facility were almost always completing class assignments or catching up with their e-mail correspondence. Likewise, the school's computer club was a conspicuously girl-free zone.

'Computer programming is fun,' insists Shannah, 'and most girls never even try it. Those who do will learn problem-solving skills that will help them in all areas of life, and they'll also have more choices in education and jobs.'

For now, the computer industry woman with the highest international profile is probably ... a doll named Barbie. Here's how to help your daughter break the mould:

- Put the family computer in a room where every interested member of the family will be able to use it. Putting it in your son's room reinforces the message that computing is a 'boy's thing'. In a mixed household, make sure your daughter has equal time on the computer, whether it's to play *Tetris*, surf the Internet, or do her homework.
- Encourage your daughter to explore the computer's full range of possibilities, rather than just using it for specific tasks and assignments. While boys tend to blame computers for computer glitches, girls tend to blame themselves. The best antidote is a sound working knowledge of computer hardware and software. Encourage your daughter to read all the right books and manuals, and give her a Philips screwdriver for her birthday.
- Seek out creative, non-competitive software like *KidPix, Storybook Weaver* or *3D Moviemaker*. And if your daughter would really rather play *CyberGladiators,* get that too.
- Many girls in their teens and pre-teens lose interest in computing because it's a solitary, introspective pursuit. It doesn't have to be. Ask your daughter to invite a few buddies around after school. Could anything be more fun than a cyber slumber party?
- If your daughter has Internet access, why not send her out for a night with the Grrls? That is, girls with Attitude, babe. Try Cybergrrls (http://www.cybergrrl.com), Webgrrls (http://www.webgrrls.com) or Geekgirls (http://www.geekgirl.com.au), all of which celebrate self-esteem, sisterhood and technological savvy in the process of having a good time online. Boys enter at their peril.
- Talk to your daughter about the possibilities of a career in computing, and the importance of computing in careers. From software development to research to programming to marketing, the opportunities are endless. Hey, someone out there has to write a better girls' program than *Barbie Fashion Designer*.

Part Three
The Internet

# Chapter 11

Sex, drugs, rock'n'roll and the Internet

Is this a nice place to bring up your kids?

Sex. Perversion. Pornography.

The way some people go on, you'd think there was nothing else out there on the Internet. But there is. Put your average Net-wise 11-year-old in front of a computer, arm him with a mouse and a modem, and leave him to his own devices. Here's the sort of bounty he might come up with in a casual half-hour of online time:

- a step-by-step recipe for making a bomb from a few simple household chemicals
- detailed instructions for picking just about any lock in business or household use
- an easy-to-use computer program for generating authentic credit card numbers at random
- 'scientific proof' that the Holocaust never happened
- an indoor farmer's guide to growing and harvesting your own marijuana plantation
- a 'Gallery of the Grotesque', featuring lurid, full-colour photographs of victims of unnatural deaths
- a Young Person's Guide to the Principles and Practices of Satanism, complete with diabolical spelling.

Shocked? You shouldn't be. This is the Internet, the most powerful medium for the free flow of information in the history of the human race. Of course, it's not entirely free. Someone has to foot the bill for those online charges and monthly service provider bills.

But the information itself — sound, text, pictures, video — is restricted only by the nerve, imagination and personal moral standards of anyone who has access to the world's most accessible computer network. The result is chaos. But it is the chaos of freedom.

Since no single person or authority controls the Internet, any official attempt to censor or regulate its content — at least in a free society — seems doomed to failure. Break down the walls! Let freedom reign! Information is the oxygen of democracy, and the Internet is a lifeline to the world.

Fine sentiments. Until the day a diversion in your travels leads you to a site that drips with venomous loathing towards blacks and Jews, or an illustrated guide to a sexual practice that seems not only inconceivable, but beyond belief. All right, so you've been educated. You're an adult.

But suddenly, in the light of what's available out there, and the complete absence of moral judgement on the part of your computer, you find yourself face-to-face with one of the biggest dilemmas of parenting in the new electronic age: how to protect your children from the Internet.

It would be wrong, indeed hysterical, to view the Internet as one huge warehouse of hate speech, subversion and hardcore pornography. Equally, it would be wrong to pretend that the Net is just a big arcade where your kids go to play games, chat with their buddies and do their homework. The truth lurks somewhere in between.

One moment you're staring open-mouthed at Hubble's latest portraits of star-clusters and exploding nebulae; the next, you're face-to-face with '250 Gorgeous Naked Babes, including Blondes, Brunettes, Lesbians and Teens' on Babes4free.Com.

One moment, you're scrolling through quotations from *Hamlet* on *The Complete Works of Shakespeare;* the next, you're engrossed in a recipe for destruction in *The Complete Terrorist's Handbook.*

Open-ended and dynamic, all-encompassing in its scope, the Internet is a reflection of life at its best and worst, the world at its ugliest and most inspiring. Where do you draw the line? In a country where the Constitution guarantees freedom of expression on any public forum, you can no longer expect the church or the state or the education system to do it for you.

It's a big and burdensome responsibility. With so much that is offensive, dangerous and degrading out there — porn on the Web, psychos on the newsgroups, perverts on IRC — you might feel tempted to put your foot down and forbid your children from going anywhere near the Internet until they turn 18.

But with so much that is good and useful out there, that would be like forbidding your children from attending school because you were worried about the traffic on the highway. Instead, you take your children by the hand, warn them about the dangers, and teach them how to cross the road.

Hopefully, they'll learn to tell left from right and right from wrong, until the day comes when you feel confident enough to let them venture forth on their own.

But what about the information highway? Let's get one thing straight. It's not a free-for-all. The Internet may like to think of itself as a working definition of anarchy, but there are certain rules that must be obeyed if the traffic of ideas and information is to flow.

Whatever else it may be, the Internet is not a passive medium for the transfer of information. In the real world, there is no danger of a young user logging on and being instantly assailed by pornography, sedition, racial hatred and all the other real and supposed evils of the Internet. You have to actively want to be assailed.

You don't have to know where you're going, but you do have to make a conscious choice, even if it is something as simple as clicking a mouse on a blue underlined hyperlink.

Having said that, just how easy is it to find the bad stuff on the Internet? The answer is simple. It's very easy, and nowhere near as easy as you might think. If that sounds like a contradiction, it's one that governs every information-gathering expedition on this vast and ever-expanding resource.

Let's join our 11-year-old as he prepares to undertake some serious research into one of the weaker subjects in his academic portfolio: Biology.

Twenty years ago, a boy of his age and curiosity might have looked up the six-letter word of his choosing in *The Oxford English Dictionary*, dog-eared the page, and passed it round the class with a snicker. Now he simply types the word into a search engine on the World Wide Web, waits a few seconds, and chooses a promising link from the dozens on offer. Click. His face falls.

Instead of 'Thousands of FREE XXX Sex Pix!', all he can see on his screen is a mass of tiny print, culminating in a legally binding declaration that 'I am at least 18 years of age, and am not offended by adult erotic material.' He thinks it over for a moment. What the heck. This is the Internet. Nobody's going to know. He clicks on YES. His face falls even further.

Now he finds himself confronted by a photograph of a smiling blonde, completely naked but for the giant Visa card between her shoulders and her knees. 'Sign up now!' says the speech bubble. 'Only $29.95 for unlimited access to the Internet's Hottest SexZone.'

He decides against it. He's got no idea where Mom keeps her credit cards. Suddenly, our 11-year-old is hit by a brainwave of the variety that somehow never hits during Biology. He types 'sex passwords' into the search engine. Bingo! In seconds, he's on his way to a top-secret site that will arm him with the codes he needs to pose as a member in good standing of dozens of adults-only sex sites. Yeah, right.

After half an hour of credit card come-ons, '404 Page Not Found' errors, and 'Incorrect password, please try again' messages, our 11-year-old gives up in disgust. There must be an easier way to do this.

He shuts down his Web browser, calls up his News Reader and connects up to a conference called alt.binaries.pictures.erotica. From the hundreds of messages on display, he clicks on 'Red-hot redhead'. He waits. And waits. Finally … wow! He can't believe his eyes. On the screen: the most incredible assembly of tightly packed letters, numbers and punctuation marks he has ever seen.

A couple of years ago, it would have taken a degree in Computer Science to turn these scrambled digits into anything resembling a red-hot redhead. Now, all it takes is a click on 'decode'. Almost instantly, the

'That doesn't look like homework to me, kid!'

binaries are converted into a high-resolution, full-colour photograph of a ... quick! Mom's back from the shops!

Deftly double-clicking, our 11-year-old shuts tell-tale windows and slips a CD-ROM into the drive. When Mom pops her head around the door, she is half-alarmed, half-relieved to see her son still sitting in the exact same position — chin in hand, shoulders hunched, eyes glued to the screen — as he studies the entry on cell division in *Microsoft Encarta*.

Such a good kid, thinks Mom. I'm so pleased I bought him that computer.

What would Mom do if she knew the terrible truth? She might pick up the phone and rant at her son's Internet service provider for making such filth freely available to innocent minors. All the company would do, of course, is declare that it is merely a conduit for the streams of data that flow through the network, and that responsibility for filtering the good bits from the bad bits must rest with the parent.

So Mom, taking that responsibility into her own hands, might unplug the modem from her son's computer and strictly forbid him from having anything more to do with that kid across the road whose father bought him a multimedia computer with an Internet connection for his birthday. Or maybe Mom will take a more reasonable approach and turn for advice to the single biggest source of wisdom and authority in the household: the Internet.

The 'filtering, monitoring and blocking' software industry, driven by concern from parents, educators, and religious and political lobby groups, is not in quite the same league as the porn by credit card industry. But it's getting there.

At last count, there were more than a dozen programs that claimed to be able to protect children from the dark side of the Internet by blocking access to certain sites, keeping a look-out for certain words and phrases, or building a secret record of a child's Internet session for later perusal by a parent or teacher.

You're unlikely to find these programs on the retail shelves — 'There's no call for them,' a hyperstore assistant assures me — but, in many cases, you'll be able to download trial versions from the Internet, with the option of an online credit card purchase if they meet your requirements. But will they? Let's take a closer look at some of the more popular programs.

Net Nanny (Net Nanny Ltd.)
WWW address: http://www.netnanny.com
As nannies go, this pioneering Internet utility appears to take its inspiration from Margaret Thatcher rather than Mary Poppins. Type a rude word, on or off the Net, and Net Nanny will instantly convert it to a series of harmless Xs.

Attempt to search on a forbidden term, or connect to a forbidden Web site or newsgroup, and Net Nanny will beep and flash a fearsome message: 'A Net Nanny violation has occurred. This program will be closed in 30 seconds.'

In more liberal-minded mode, Net Nanny will merely note than an 'unacceptable word or phrase has been detected', and will dutifully record the violation in its password-protected log.

Although the program comes with a predefined list of sites deemed undesirable for minors — from www.bigtits.com to alt.personals.jewish — the onus is on the parent to set the limits of acceptability.

This is a fine principle, but it does mean you're going to have to put some effort into researching and visiting the sites you wouldn't want your own children to visit. You can also define a list of forbidden words and phrases, including personal information such as addresses, telephone numbers and credit card numbers.

Net Nanny is a highly visible and vigilant deterrent to unsafe surfing, but it does have its irritations. When I tried it out, it repeatedly sensed evil lurking in wholly innocent places, such as the Rockwell modem upgrade site, where it insisted that 'mcd' was an unacceptable word or phrase. It also wielded its Xs with terrifying zeal at the Pointcast news-gathering site, where a mundane paragraph on software licensing was reduced to a string of hardcore gibberish.

None of the words in question had been defined in the program's database, so perhaps this nanny, like all good nannies, was simply erring on the side of propriety.

Cyber Patrol (Microsystems Software)
WWW address: http://www.cyberpatrol.com
'To surf and protect', pledges Cyber Patrol, the Internet blocking program that's more than an Internet blocking program. Aside from controlling your child's access to the various areas of the Internet, it also allows you to restrict time spent online and at the computer as a whole.

You can block up to eight Windows applications, such as games or financial software, and you can even track attempts to bypass or shut down Cyber Patrol itself.

You can prevent your child from transmitting any sensitive personal information over a chat line, or from joining any IRC chat channels of a dubious nature. Is there anything the program allows you to do?

Yes: You're allowed access to any site on the CyberYES list, as rated by a panel of parents and educators, and you can also customise or adjust the CyberNOT list to suit the age or maturity levels of up to ten users.

Cyber Patrol's definitions of what's YES and what's NOT are detailed to an almost pathological degree. The 12 categories range from Violence/Profanity to Gross Depictions to Militant/Extremist, with a balance carefully drawn between the need to safeguard children and the need to keep them informed.

In the category of Sex Education, for instance, Cyber Patrol allows access to 'pictures or text advocating the proper use of contraceptives', but not to 'commercial sites wishing to sell sexual paraphernalia'.

With its wide range of options and exceptions, Cyber Patrol is easily the most flexible and efficient blocking program on the block. Well, maybe 'easily' is the wrong word: This is not a program for anyone who is put off by screen after screen of little boxes that need to be checked or unchecked.

Cyber Patrol won't solve all your Internet access concerns, but it is highly recommended for households where dishwashing agendas and television-watching timetables routinely find a place on the refrigerator door.

CYBERSITTER (SOLID OAK SOFTWARE)
WWW address: http://www.cybersitter.com

Cybersitter is the secret agent of Internet blocking programs. It sits in the background, unannounced and unnoticed, quietly observing, logging and laying down the law according to Mom and Dad.

Search on a forbidden topic, and Cybersitter won't yell at you: It'll simply return you to the search engine without a single response. Head for a forbidden site on the Web, Internet Relay Chat (IRC) or Usenet, and you'll get nothing but an ambiguous and totally unhelpful error message. So far, so fine.

But Cybersitter does have some very odd habits that can make it seem, at times, more like a gremlin than a proxy for parental guidance. For instance, the program has a propensity for blanking out words it doesn't want your children to see.

Just how rigidly this policy is enforced became apparent when I saw the following headline on a Web news page: 'Million pected to Explore the Red Planet Online'. Should've been 'Millions Expected', of course, but Cybersitter didn't like the way three of those little letters added up to sex.

Weirder still are the parameters Cybersitter uses to block or allow access to information. You can visit sites about Ecstasy, but not marijuana. You can learn all about contraception, but not condoms.

Not surprisingly, Cybersitter won't allow you to search on 'sexuality', but if you try the exact opposite — 'asexual reproduction' (a staple of the high school Biology curriculum) — your search term will be truncated to a single letter 'a'.

Okay, so what about an innocent word like, let's say, 'chicken'? Forget it. Cybersitter gets as far as 'chick' before putting up the barricades. Same goes for 'babe'. Even if you only mean the pig in the movie.

Then again, Cybersitter has no problems with 'fart', or, more tellingly, 'Satanism', allowing unfettered access to dozens of online documents about the theory and practice of devil-worship.

Although you can add your own sites, words and phrases to Cybersitter's vast and un-editable database, the overriding impression is one of vigilance and political correctness taken too far. I seriously believe this program needs to see a shrink.

SurfWatch (SpyGlass Inc.)
WWW address: http://www.surfwatch.com
Sex, drugs, alcohol, gambling, hate speech and gratuitous violence fall under SurfWatch's watchful eye, but the program's vigilance is tempered with an unusually high degree of tolerance.

Most blocking programs, by default, won't allow a search on the once-innocent word 'gay'; SurfWatch will let you go ahead, but will keep you from entering areas it deems explicit or obscene.

Likewise, the program allows you to research the effects of mind-altering chemicals, but blocks access to the pro-drug pages of *High Times* magazine. Depending on what you want from an Internet blocking program, this kind of latitude is either a major strength or an unforgivable weakness.

SurfWatch allows only limited customisation of its list of filters, which apply to the Web, newsgroups, and FTP and IRC sites, but the program's big plus is its ease of operation.

It installs painlessly and stays out of the way until an inappropriate site triggers a no-entry sign or a 'blocked by SurfWatch' message. An unusually open-minded option for parents of older kids, even if it does occasionally appear to defeat its own purpose.

Cyber Snoop (Pearl Software Inc.)
WWW address: http://www.pearlsw.com
Far and away the most ruthlessly effective Internet blocking program I have ever come across, albeit for the wrong reasons. An inadvertent click during installation caused Cyber Snoop to replace a vital Windows 95 file — something called winsock.dll — with an update of its own.

Result: Like a bouncer at a trendy nightclub, my Web browser simply refused to allow me access. It was only after much snooping around of my own that I was able to fix the glitch and try again. So what does Cyber Snoop do when it isn't performing invasive surgery on your operating system? Well, it snoops.

Although the program allows you to restrict Internet access according to your own criteria, its real function is to hover in the background and keep tabs on what your child is getting up to on the information highway.

Every click, link, file transfer and e-mail message is recorded in a detailed activity log, allowing you to recreate the session and, presumably, present your offspring with indisputable evidence that 'this does not look like homework to me'.

Easy to operate, as long as you keep your eyes peeled during installation, Cyber Snoop is recommended for parents who feel uneasy about censorship, but have no qualms about keeping their kids under surveillance.

So? Are these programs the definitive answer to the perils of the Net? Can you install one or more and safely leave your child to surf in friendly and inviting waters? Hmmm. I don't think so.

Internet blocking programs — no one dares to call them Internet censoring programs — are flawed in many ways, not the least of which is the central paradox under which they operate. Any kid who knows enough about the Internet to need protection from it is going to know enough about the Internet to be able to bypass that protection.

A simple example: It took me no more than ten minutes, using an Internet search engine, to find an easy and undetectable way of disabling *Net Nanny*, *Cyber Patrol* and *Cybersitter*. And I'm not even 11. Even if the programs were childproof — and future versions may well be — what's to stop your kid from trying out all those explicitly forbidden sites on a computer that isn't blocked?

In any case, even the most vigilant and frequently updated blocking programs will never be able to keep all of the Net's 'inappropriate' sites at bay. Something, somewhere, sooner or later, is going to slip through the Net. With this in mind, you may want to try the other Great Hope for a Child-Safe Internet: voluntary ratings.

Using criteria provided by two main organisations, SafeSurf (http://www.safesurf.com) and the Recreational Software Advisory Council (http://www.rsac.org), content-providers and Web administrators are encouraged to rate their sites as a way of staving off the prospect of government legislation.

The ratings are encoded into the sites themselves, making it easy for filtering programs to seek out appropriate material for younger users. If you're using Internet Explorer as your Web browser, you can put this to the test right now by clicking on View, then Options, then Security, then Enable Ratings.

You'll be prompted for a 'supervisor's password', following which you'll be able to define your own levels of acceptability for Violence, Nudity, Sex and Language. Thus enabled, the browser can access only those sites that have been encoded with the appropriate ratings.

It's a good idea, based on the 'can go' rather than the 'can't go' principle of Internet access, but its time hasn't come — yet. Of the estimated 60 million sites on the Web, only a couple of hundred thousand have taken up the invitation to rate their content. This means that your kids won't just be protected from the bad stuff; they'll also be denied access to millions of wholesome, fun and educational sites that haven't been rated yet.

Until the voluntary ratings system gains more support, or becomes mandatory — highly unlikely, given the lack of a central authority on the Internet — the real responsibility for safeguarding kids online will lie elsewhere.

Parents will need to accept that the Internet has a dark side; that it is not just a medium of communication, but a community in itself, made up of people who are good, bad and indifferent, noble, caring and malicious.

Parents will need to acquaint their children with the dangers and the diversity of life on the Net to encourage a healthy sense of scepticism and a readiness to pull the plug on anything or anyone that doesn't seem right.

Parents will need to strike a balance between close supervision and control, and acceptance of the fact that today's children are growing up in a different world: a boundless environment characterised by freedom of thought, speech and deed.

More than anything else, parents will need to look beyond the hype and hysteria to realise that the Internet, for all its human flaws and failings, is not something that can simply be rated XXX and banished from public life. Instead, it must be rated PG. And that's where you come in.

Chapter 12

50 weird, wacky and wonderful things for kids (and their parents) to do on the World Wide Web

Read all the news that's fit to print in *The New York Times*. Study the masterpieces of the Renaissance in the Louvre. Follow the painstaking progress of the first manned mission to Mars. Learn the words to 'Nkosi Sikele'l iAfrika'.

Whatever your interest or obsession, you'll find a home for it on the Internet's busiest thoroughfare: the World Wide Web. But there's more to the Web than hard work, solid information and practical resources for academic research. There's nonsense. There's serendipity. There's fun, ephemera and mindlessness of the most mind-numbing variety. As the most free-spirited forum in the history of publishing, the Web is as willing to accommodate a doctoral dissertation on nuclear physics as it is a digitally sampled collection of rude body noises.

A mouse-click away from the serious stuff, you can find out everything you never wanted to know about nose-picking, watch a pot of coffee brewing on a tabletop at Cambridge University, or leave a personal message for someone's cat. Why? Because you can.

Click-start your Web browser, and set the controls for the following hand-picked sites. *Note:* At the time of writing (1.27 pm), all of the following links were active and working. Given the dynamic, constantly shifting nature of the Web, however, this may not be so by the time you try them out. In which case, type the relevant keywords into your trusty Internet search engine, and it'll point you in the right direction.

1. Take a ride in the world's ultimate taxi
WWW address: http://www.ultimatetaxi.com
Somewhere in the cool streets of Aspen, Colorado, Jon Barnes is taking someone for a ride. But this is no ordinary taxi. This is ... CyberTaxi!

Wired to the world by laptop and cellular phone, lit up by disco lights and a spinning mirror-ball, this transport of delight will take you on a trip to another dimension.

2. Get inside the skin of a cockroach
WWW address: http://www.nj.com/yucky/roaches/index.html
Hey, did you know that the skeleton of a cockroach is on the outside of its body? This and many other fascinating facts await the unwary on what is proudly dubbed 'the yuckiest site on the Internet'.

3. Juggle the family crockery
WWW address: http://www.hal.com/services/juggle/help/
Begin with Ping-Pong balls, move on to China plates, graduate to flaming torches. Everything you wanted to know about getting the breaks in juggling.

4. Find out if you're a vampire
WWW address: http://www.vampyre.wis.net/vampyre/index.html
Just because you're allergic to garlic doesn't mean you're a bloodsucking creature of the night. Get your teeth into this checklist to see if you really fit the bill.

5. Dissect a virtual frog
WWW address: http://george.lbl.gov/vfrog/
For the squeamish but curious, an excellent opportunity to examine the innards of an amphibian.

6. Dissect a virtual human
WWW address:
http://www.nlm.nih.gov/extramural_research.dir/photos.html
The marvels of human anatomy laid bare, in the world's first digitally photographed autopsy. (They used the body of an executed prisoner.)

7. Tell the time in foam bath fish
WWW address: http://www.northcoast.com/cgi-bin/fishtime?-6
'I had a whale of a time, but what's the porpoise?' asks one visitor to this popular site, which displays the current time in a line-up of numbered foam bath fish.

8. Make your own recycled paper
WWW address: http://www.nbn.com/youcan/paper/paper.html
A messy recipe for saving a tree using nothing but glue, water, an electric iron, a food processor, a pair of old pantyhose and a couple of pages from yesterday's newspaper.

9. Ask a dog to do your Maths homework
WWW address: http://kao.ini.cmu.edu:5550/bdf.html
Who needs a calculator when you've got Blue Dog, the canine mathematical marvel of the Internet? Just type in your formula, no matter how complicated, and Blue Dog will faithfully bark the answer.

10. Fake an alien invasion
WWW address:
http://www.strw.leidenuniv.nl/~vdmeulen/Articles/UFOfake.html
Any earthling can throw a hubcap into the air and snap a blurry picture for the eight o'clock news. But if you really want to cause panic in the streets, try these handy ... on second thoughts, maybe it's not such a good idea. Hey! Great! This site also teaches you how to make your very own alien crop circle!

11. Take a tour of the sun
WWW address: http://www.astro.uva.nl/michielb/od95/
Set the controls for a fascinating journey to the hottest site in the solar system.

12. Give Xavier the Robot a task to perform
WWW address: http://jubilee.learning.cs.cmu.edu:8080/command.html
Xavier is the resident hunk of scrap metal and exposed wiring at the Robotics Institute of the Carnegie Mellon University in America. Give him a command from the pre-defined list, and watch him get to work — willing slave to a computer on the other side of the planet.

13. Learn how to skin the cat
WWW address: http://www.li.net/~autorent/yo-yo.htm
Don't worry — it's a yo-yo trick. Plenty of others, too, guaranteed to turn even the most fumble-fingered kid into a nimble king of string.

14. Spy on an iguana
WWW address: http://iguana.images.com/
Somewhere on the other side of the world someone's pet iguana remains blissfully unaware that a camera attached to a computer is transmitting its image to millions of Internet users with nothing better to do.

15. Operate an interactive model railroad
WWW address: http://rr-vs.informatik.uni-ulm.de/rr/
Thanks to a group of bored but brilliant boffins at the University of Ulm, you can now use your powerful multimedia computer to make a toy train go right off the rails — live and on video before your very eyes. What will they think of next?

16. Learn how to survive a moray eel attack
WWW address: http://www.woodwind.com/mtlake/CyberKids/Issue4/SeaCreatures/Underwater.html
When morays bite, they don't let go. So don't pull. What you have to do is 'distract the moray with something more attractive to eat'. If that doesn't work, just break its jaw.

17. Find out everything you ever wanted to know about sleep, but were too tired to ask
WWW address: http://bisleep.medsch.ucla.edu/Default.html
The inside story on the world's favourite pastime. Zzzzzzz...

18. Go on patrol with the LAPD Blue
WWW address: http://www.policescanner.com
'Sqrwk xblksqnrrrxxx on vcxgschhhbn and mmmnnnplkx, Car 23. Come in please.'

'Xcvwwwfg grrrrnt xzneeeow. Ngbsfxc on Hollywood and Vine. Brrrbllglmph. Roger.'

It may sound like Klingons in conversation off the shoulder of Orion, but it's really something more exciting: police dispatchers communicating with patrol officers *en route* to real-life Los Angeles crime scenes. Truly one of the Web's most ear-boggling sites. To appreciate it in full, you'll need to download a nifty little plug-in program called Real Audio (go to http://www.realaudio.com).

19. See the world through Steve Mann's eyes
WWW address:
http://www-white.media.mit.edu/%7Esteve/html9/myviews.html
Steve Mann? Oh, he's just some guy who wanders around all day with a 'Webcamera' strapped to his head. Then he puts the pictures on the Internet for all to see. Why? Well, how else is he supposed to explain that camera on his head?

20. Send a friend an electric postcard
WWW address: http://postcards.www.media.mit.edu/Postcards/
Having a nice time in cyberspace? Tell a pal by sending a virtual postcard over the wire. No stamp required.

21. Say Happy Birthday to a total stranger
WWW address: http://www.boutell.com/birthday.cgi/
Spread a little random cheer by sending birthday greetings to the friend or stranger of your choice on the Birthday Web. Then add your e-mail address and birth date to the list, and wait for the messages to roll in.

50 weird, wacky and wonderful things for kids to do on the World Wide Web 121

22. Learn to converse in Klingon
WWW address: http://www.abdn.ac.uk/~u06rmm/Terran.html
It may not have made the school curriculum yet, but Klingon is one of the galaxy's most widely-spoken tongues. At least on *Star Trek*. Q'Apla!

23. Make your own atomic bomb
WWW address:
http://www.student.nada.kth.se/~nv91-asa/atomic.html
Don't worry, parents. It's nowhere near as easy as it sounds. For starters, few pharmacies keep a ready supply of uranium-235 on the shelves. But for enquiring minds that just have to know what makes a thermonuclear device go boom, this is the place to look.

24. Take the Nerd Test
WWW address: http://gonzo.tamu.edu/nerd.html
Do you know what 'WYSIWYG' stands for? Have you ever done homework on a Friday night? Does your underwear have your name in it? Do you enjoy answering pointless questionnaires on the Internet? Try this one then.

25. Take a tour of the world's only online barfbag museum
WWW address: http://www.tns.lcs.mit.edu/~izzy/barfbag.html
What do you call a guy who collects air sickness bags? And then actually puts them on the Internet for all to see? Could be worse. At least they're not *used* air sickness bags...

26. Make a paper dragon
WWW address: http://www.cs.ubc.ca/spider/jwu/origami.html
Until the paperless society becomes a reality, you may as well find a use for all that scrap paper lying around the house. Origami is it.

27. Learn how to care for your tarantula
WWW address: http://www.ex.ac.uk/~gjlramel/tarantul.html
Warning! Never, ever disturb a tarantula while it's moulting. Find out why on this splendidly spidery site.

28. Create your own newspaper
WWW address: http://crayon.net/
Tick the little boxes to make your own personalised gateway to the news of the world and the wonders of the World Wide Web.

29. Join the Fruit-of-the-Day Club
WWW address: http://www.cs.umd.edu/~mike/fruit-of-the-day.html
And today's fruit is ... the guava. Tomorrow's will be something completely different, just as yesterday's was. Why should anyone have to settle for an apple every day?

30. Party with the plastic princess
WWW address http://www.primenet.com/~jesica/index.html
She's blonde, she's beautiful, she's 100 per cent non-biodegradable. Little girls of all ages will flip for this, the Internet's ultimate Barbie site.

31. See the world's first dinosaur skeleton
WWW address: http://www.levins.com/xdinosaur.html
In the summer of 1858, a Victorian gentleman named William Parker Foulke found the bones of a creature larger than an elephant, with the structural features of a lizard and a bird, in a slime pit in Haddonfield, New Jersey. Now you can see it too — without getting all covered in slime.

32. Find out if it's raining in space
WWW address: http://www.sel.bldrdoc.gov/today.html
Planning a trip to another part of the solar system? Before you pack, check the weather out there on this useful site from America's Space Environment Centre. Sample forecast: 'The geomagnetic field is expected to be unsettled for the next three days, with isolated periods of active conditions likely.' And you thought they didn't have weather in space.

33. Check out the surf in Santa Barbara
WWW address: http://www.sdsc.edu/surf/surfsup.html
After a hard day's surfing on the Internet, it's nice to know that — depending on surf patterns and weather conditions — the people of Santa Barbara, California, are just getting ready to surf on the ocean. Apply here for your daily surf report, delivered free of charge to your e-mail address.

34. Master the art of the Shakespearean insult
WWW address: http://www.nova.edu/Inter-Links/cgi-bin/bard.pl
'Surrender, thou frothy guts-griping apple-john!' To which the suggested reply is: 'Never, thou goatish hasty-witted whey-face!' A different insult from the Bard's bottomless repertoire every time you press the reload button on your browser.

35. Get the complete script of *The Lion King*
WWW address: http://www.pionet.net/~mcginnr/tlktext.html
Worried that your kids don't know every single word of *The Lion King*, despite having seen it umpteen-million times? *Hakuna matata*. It's all here, along with a whole bunch of other regally leonine stuff to keep them occupied when the TV's switched off.

36. Take a fantastic voyage through your computer
WWW address: http://www.att.com/microscapes/microscapes.html
There's a world of mystery, beauty and wonder hiding inside the tiniest computer chip, as revealed by these awesome images from the Microscape Gallery.

37. Make your own solar cooker
WWW address: http://www.accessone.com/~sbcn/plans.htm
Who needs a microwave when you've got a home-made parabolic-dish cooking contraption? Just the thing for that next power failure in sunny South Africa.

38. Listen to the song of the humpback whale
WWW address: http://www.sfu.ca/~michaec/whales.htm
Explore the enigmatic underwater world of this renegade among ocean dwellers, in sound, video and 3-D graphics. One of the best whale sites on the Web.

39. Exercise your IQ
WWW address: http://www.miracle.com/mensa/workout.cgi
'If it were two hours later, it would be half as long until midnight as it would be if it were an hour later. What time is it now?' If you can make any sense of the question, let alone the answer, you may be eligible for membership of Mensa, the club for people who think they're clever.

40. Say a few words to the automatic talking machine
WWW address: http://www.inference.com/~hansen/talk.html
Type in a sentence or two, click on 'Say It', and your words will be spoken aloud in the office of a major computer nut in San Francisco. Remember, this is a major breakthrough in cyber-communication, so try to think of something more meaningful than 'Yebo, Gogo'.

41. Find a better mousetrap
WWW address: http://colitz.com/site/wacky.htm
An automatic saluting device? An audible toothbrush? A combined grater, slicer, and mouse- and flytrap? All these and more on 'Wacky Patent of the Month', a site that pays due homage to the mother of invention.

50 weird, wacky and wonderful things for kids to do on the World Wide Web

42. Take a virtual tour of a Boeing 727 cockpit
WWW address:
http://www.net-works.net/community/msd/727index.htm
Hey! Don't touch that dial! On second thoughts, go right ahead. It's only virtual.

43. Order a pizza by e-mail
WWW address: http://www2.ecst.csuchico.edu/~pizza/
When all that surfing leaves you feeling peckish, order a pizza with all the toppings and have it delivered straight to your mailbox. Is it a real pizza? Of course! Down to the very last byte.

44. See what a pumpkin looks like when it's dropped down a ten-storey stairwell
WWW address: http://www.dropsquad.com/
Centuries ago, some guy dropped a feather and an iron ball from the top of the Tower of Pisa to demonstrate some scientific principle or other. But he couldn't have had anywhere near as much fun as the Drop Squad of the Carnegie Mellon University, who hurl typewriters, vinyl records, coffee pots and hamburgers from the top of their stairwell, for no other reason than to see what a mess it makes.

45. Surprise your eyes
WWW address: http://lainet3.lainet.com/~ausbourn/jumplist.htm
Jeepers creepers, you won't believe your peepers. An incredible collection of optical illusions through the ages.

46. Unravel the mystery of the Main Sanitary Nag
WWW address: http://www.infobahn.com/pages/anagram.html
All right, it's no great mystery: 'Main Sanitary Nag' is an anagram of Anagram Insanity, a site that offers instant and often revealing anagrams of your name, your home town or any phrase you care to enter. Fishy rung pap! (Happy surfing.)

47. Take an incredible journey to the far side of the universe
WWW address: http://www.seds.org/hst/
From the Dusky Disk of Beta Pictoris to the nucleus of the Whirlpool Galaxy, from volcanoes on Io to sunset on Saturn's rings, a choice

selection of snapshots from Hubble's interplanetary album. Probably the only site on the Internet that truly deserves to be called 'awesome'.

48. Join the club for people who've memorised 1 000 digits of Pi
WWW address: http://www.ts.umu.se/~olletg/pi/club_1000.html
If you have to ask what 'Pi' is, apply elsewhere. Otherwise, simply jot down those digits in an e-mail message — from memory, of course! — and join the Internet's most exclusive circle of supernerds. Easy as Pi.

49. Find out how far it is from here to there
WWW address: http://www.indo.com/distance/
Enter the names of any two cities, and the distance between them will be revealed in a flash. But you'll have to be specific: Did you know there are four Johannesburgs in the world?

50. Press the big red button that doesn't do anything
WWW address: http://www.wam.umd.edu/~twoflowr/button.htm
Go on, press it. It doesn't do anything. No, really ... just press it. And don't say you haven't been warned.

Chapter 13

How to find out everything you ever wanted to know about anything on the Internet

Knowledge is of two kinds. We know a subject ourselves, or we know where we can find information upon it.
            SAMUEL JOHNSON, LEXICOGRAPHER, APRIL 1775

Help! Your three-year-old has just been bitten by a snake. At least, that's what your three-year-old says.

All attempts to elicit further information — 'Where is the snake? How big was it? Was it a highly venomous Egyptian Cobra or a relatively harmless mole snake?' — are met with red-faced howls of agony and frantic clutching of the affected limb or digit. There's only one thing to do. Panic.

But even as you flip your frenzied fingers through the phone book, trying to find 'Emergency Services' under 'Government Departments', the thought might occur: Wonder if there's anything about this on the Internet? Good call.

Everyone knows you can find out everything you ever wanted to know about anything you never even knew you needed to know on the Internet. All you have to do is start your Web browser, surf on over to the search engine of your choice, type a few words into the little box on screen, click on Search or Enter, and sit back as your computer miraculously wades through millions of online documents to bring back precisely the titbit of information you require.

Well, that's the theory. In practice, trying to find information on the Internet is a little like trying to find hay in a haystack. Sure, you can dive right in and come out all covered in hay. But what if you're looking for a specific piece of hay? What if you're looking for a needle? You get the point.

On the Internet, you have to know not just what you're looking for, but exactly where and how to find it. Parents, if there's one really valuable skill you can teach your children in the Age of the Internet, aside from how to remove those little bits of popcorn that get stuck inside a keyboard, it's how to become an expert hunter and gatherer of information. (Knowing what to do with the information once you've found it is a different story. We'll get on to it.)

But we digress. This is an emergency. As the howls of your snake-bitten toddler continue to pierce the air, one question will most likely be uppermost in your mind. What's a search engine?

Spiders, robots and crawlers

Simply put, a search engine is a Web site or service designed to help you make some sort of sense of the Internet. Using a powerful piece of software known as a 'robot', 'crawler' or 'Web spider', search engines travel the highways and byways of cyberspace at enormous speed, seeking out, collating, indexing, updating, storing and retrieving megabytes of useful and useless information for your perusal.

To be precise, a search engine will not present you with actual information. What it will do is point you in the right direction, by providing a list of clickable links to sites that may or may not match your requirements.

Search engines are integral to the successful utilisation of the Internet. Without them, we'd be stranded. With them, we'd be stranded too if we didn't know exactly how to make them do our bidding. For the truth is they're pretty useless when it comes to reading minds.

Let's say you're on a hunt for everything and anything to do with 'beetles' on the Internet. You know perfectly well that you mean the VW bug variety. But what does your search engine bring you? Pages and pages of detailed information about insects of the order Coleopteran. That's because you neglected to specify that you were looking for 'VW Beetles', as opposed to 'beetles insects'. Search engines make excellent detectives, but they need all the clues they can get. It's easy when you know how. First, find yourself a search engine.

There are plenty to choose from, with wild variations in size, scope, sophistication and prettiness of design. You'll find two basic flavours: the 'query-based' model, where you type in a word or phrase and await a flood of responses; and the slower but more structured 'topic directory', where you take control of the search by drilling down through layers of information until you find exactly what you think you've been looking for.

Try any one of the following search engines for size. On second thoughts, try them all. They're free!

AltaVista
WWW address: http://www.altavista.digital.com/
A superfast, industrial-strength search engine that takes pride in ferreting out information from the most obscure corners of the Web. Many users swear by it; others find its range too sweeping for comfort.

Excite
WWW address: http://www.excite.com/
A slightly slower but flexible information finder that draws on a database of 50-million sites. Also offers crisp and informative reviews of selected new sites.

HotBot
WWW address: http://www.hotbot.com
A hip, hot and highly customisable gateway to the wonders of the Web — and beyond.

Infoseek Guide
WWW address: http://www.infoseek.com/
A smart and user-friendly amalgam of four separate search engines. Its best feature is that it allows you to phrase queries in plain English.

LookSmart
WWW address: http://www.looksmart.com
Run by Reader's Digest, this family-oriented facility cuts the smut and trims the Web to its lean but muscular essentials. Useful if you're worried about rude responses to seemingly innocent queries.

Magellan
WWW address: http://www.mckinley.com/
Trading speed for focus, this intelligent directory offers helpful ratings and a facility to filter out sites deemed unsuitable for younger users.

MetaCrawler
WWW address:
http://metacrawler.cs.washington.edu:8080/home.html
If you really want to know it all, put your question to this weighty oracle, which will in turn interrogate eight of the Web's most powerful search engines.

Yahoo!
WWW address: http://www.yahoo.com
The grand-daddy of Internet search engines, boasting a subject directory compiled and updated by actual humans.

Yahooligans!
WWW address: http://www.yahooligans.com
Same as Yahoo!, only brighter, funkier and aimed at information seekers aged 15 and under.

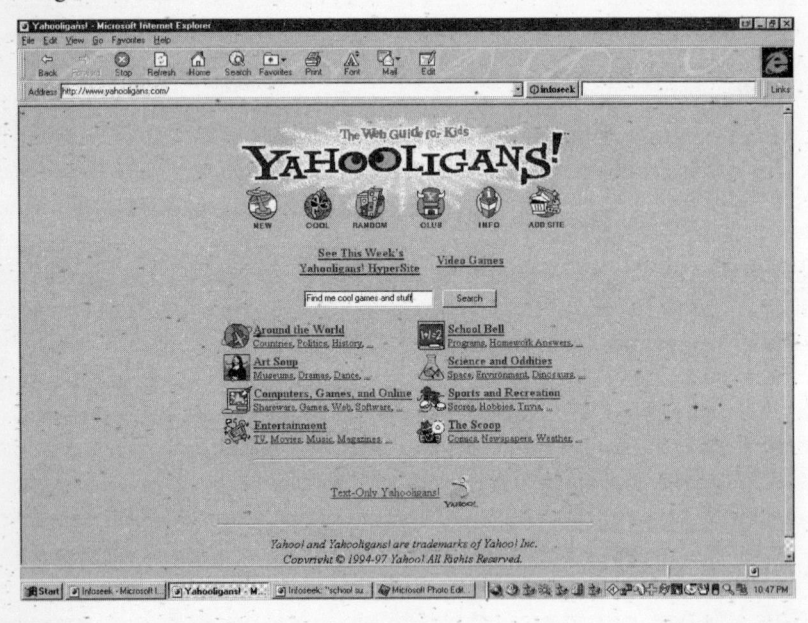

As you'll discover, each search engine has its own virtues and idiosyncrasies. Whichever one you choose, it's important to remember that searching the Net is not just a process. It's a science and an art, requiring planning, patience and a fair degree of intuition. Small wonder that the cry most commonly heard from new users on the Net is: 'Help! I can't find anything in here!'

Define, refine, search, research

Your cry has been heard. Here is my magical four-step formula for searching the Net:

1. **Define** Before you even connect, get a good grip on exactly what it is you're looking for.
2. **Refine** Narrow your parameters and zoom in on essentials.
3. **Search** Enter your query and sift through the results.
4. **Research** Search again, defining and refining until you reach your goal. Then do your research.

Here's how it works. Say you're searching for helpful information on, let's see, snakebites. What's the first word that springs to mind? 'Help', of course, followed closely by 'snakes'. So you type that word into the little white box on the Excite site. What do you get? Snakes.

Everything from the rules of snakes and ladders to the feeding and care of American Pit Vipers to the official home page of the Impotent Sea Snakes (a heavy metal band). But very little about bites.

Now this is fine if you're just browsing. Serendipitous discovery is one of the joys of Internet life. But if you really want to cut through the morass and drill right down to the nitty-gritty, what you have to do is *define* your search.

The keyword is … keywords. Anything that springs to mind, as long as it's connected to your quest. In this case, since you're dealing with an emergency that happens to involve a snakebite, and you're desperately seeking advice on treatment, a good starting-point would be 'emergency snakebite treatment'. (Leave off the inverted commas. They're only used if you want to find a string of words in exact sequence, such as 'Truth and Reconciliation Commission' or 'rules of snakes and ladders'.) Now let's type our phrase into a few random search engines, and see where it leads us:

Infoseek This site allows querying in plain English so we could phrase our question as, 'How do I treat a suspected venomous snakebite wound?' But we just don't have the time for proper sentence construction. Instead, within seconds, our breathless lowercase query — emergency snakebite treatment — generates a staggering 427 733 responses.

Fortunately, as is the custom with search engines, the links are listed in order of relevance, ten to a page. Because computers can't judge relevance as well as humans, we still need to scan the summaries for the most likely-sounding candidates:

- The Netvet Reptile home page? Nope. We're not interested in sick snakes.
- The Costa Rica Medicinal Plant Project? Nope. It's in Spanish.
- The Herpmed: Medical Herpetology site? Yes! Whatever 'herpetology' means, the words 'snakebite' and 'venom' leap out like a forked tongue, so we click on the link, and it takes us to a site with more links to click on. Reptilian salmonella, Rattlesnake Information Database ... ah: The Snakebite Emergency First-Aid Page. Click.

HotBot Having instructed the engine to search for 'all the words' in our query (as opposed to 'any of the words' or 'exact phrase'), we send it off on its mission of mercy. Result: a frugal but focused 143 matches, many related to tales of outdoor adventure and safari holiday recommendations.

But right near the top, we have the highly promising 'Snakebite Injury Gallery'. Turns out to be an illustrated chapter from an online medical encyclopaedia. What? You're *not* supposed to try and suck out the venom through your teeth?

AltaVista Phew! Living up to its reputation as the Web's widest and speediest searcher, AltaVista barely blinks before presenting us with some 600 000 opportunities for further investigation. Top of the list is a commercial site for 'Snakebite Treatment Supplies'. We're not buying. But 'Snakebite Emergency First-Aid Information' sounds right up our alley.

A single click leads to a special feature on snakes and bites in the metropolitan section of *The Boston Globe*. A little far from the tropics, perhaps, but the opening advice is right on the button: 'Do not panic.'

The moral? Well, contrary to popular belief, we've proved that it is possible to extract precise, pertinent information from the Internet in a hurry. That AltaVista search took less than 20 seconds from query to resolution. (Warning: Results will vary according to modem and processor speed, time of day and your ability to scan Web sites for keywords without actually reading.)

But this is only the beginning. To unleash the real power of info-searching on the Internet, you have to teach that little robot to focus with the intensity of a laser beam. You have to *refine* your search, and then *refine* some more. How you do this will depend on which search engine you choose but, as a general rule, you'll be calling on the power of the Boolean Operators. Don't worry — they're not a heavy metal band.

The Boolean method

Boolean Operators (named after George Boole, mathematician) are nothing more than little words that have to be typed in big letters. For example: 'AND', 'AND NOT', 'WITH', 'NEAR' and 'OR'. By incorporating these words into your search query, you instruct the search engine to include or exclude certain categories of information. Result: a search that delivers the goods with pinpoint accuracy.

Let's say you've developed a sudden interest in African herpetology. You're convinced there is a python on the loose somewhere in your household. Looking over your shoulder, you type the word 'python' into your search engine. What do you get? Zillions of documents about the Monty Python comedy troupe and a computer programming language called Python. Time to refine.

Try this: python AND african AND NOT monty (exact syntax, please). See the difference? The very first link takes you to a splendid picture of an African Burrowing Python in the act of murdering a rat. That's because you ordered the search engine to search for all adjacent instances of 'African' and 'python', while excluding all references to 'Monty'.

Likewise, if you really wanted to know how to program in Python, you would phrase your query thus: python AND NOT snakes AND NOT monty. But maybe you're beginning to suspect that your reptilian intruder could just as easily be a cobra. No problem. Search for: snakes AND (cobras OR pythons). The brackets instruct your search engine to group specific sub-categories of information under an umbrella category.

Speaking of snakes and medical emergencies, haven't you always wanted to know the origin and meaning of that little pharmaceutical symbol with the two serpents entwined around a shepherd's staff? It's called a 'caduceus', as you'll learn by diverting your search to snakes AND medicine AND symbol.

As you'll see, the permutations are endless. And if you thought your Standard 3 English grammar teacher was heavy on syntax, you ain't seen nothing yet. (Sorry, Mrs Piggot.) For instance, some search engines allow you to use a '–' or '+' sign in place of the Boolean Operators.

Example: +'and now for something completely different' +monty –wanda. This would return a horde of Monty Python sites containing the exact phrase in inverted commas, while leaving out any that refer to *A Fish Called Wanda*.

By now, of course, you will have completely forgotten about the herpetological crisis at hand. Relax. Turns out it wasn't a snake after all, but a shongololo that fell from a tree and brushed your toddler on the arm. Hmmm ... wonder if there's anything about shongololos on the Internet?

You bet. But before you set off on your merry, meandering way, here's the bottom line. No matter how carefully you define and refine your search, searching isn't the same as researching. And no matter how much information you unearth, information isn't the same as knowledge.

Learning to tell the difference is what turns the Internet from a giant warehouse of raw, unfiltered data into a practical tool for empowering and enlightening your children. Sounds like hard work. Let's have a little fun instead.

Let's have a search party!
A fun-filled, fact-finding game for the whole family

What is the capital of Uzbekistan? How many bones are there in the human body? Who was the fifteenth president of the United States? How do you do the Macarena? Where was the Treaty of Versailles signed? Why can't you tickle yourself?

Yes, life is full of questions. And as a parent, you're expected to know all the answers. But don't just hand them to your children on a plate.

Tempting as it may be, don't just point them in the direction of the Great Electronic Oracle, either. The Internet doesn't know it all. Or worse — maybe it does.

Here's a little exercise that will help put that equation to the test. It will also sharpen information-gathering skills, build up your compendium of general knowledge, and give the whole family something to do on a grey and rainy day when the video-machine isn't working.

What you'll need:
- a computer with Internet access
- a willing line-up of kids and adults with varying degrees of computer literacy
- a wide selection of hard-copy reference sources in conventional analogue format, that is to say, books
- a bunch of newspapers, magazines and other printed stuff
- paper to scribble on
- a variety of perplexing questions about life, the universe and everything
- snacks — just keep them far away from the keyboard, okay?

Now divide the family into two teams, one logged on to the World Wide Web, and the other restricted to all the printed material they can lay their hands on. Each team takes turns to pose questions, ranging from the pedestrian to the outrageously obscure. The object is to track down the correct answer in the shortest possible time.

Let's start with the easy-as-pie 'how many bones in the human body' conundrum. Er, 312, right? Or thereabouts. The race is on.

Pulses pounding, Team A peruses a shelf-ful of hefty encyclopaedias. Will they find the answer under A for Anatomy, B for Bones, or S for Skeleton? As the precious milliseconds tick by, Team B rushes over to http://www.infoseek.com and formats a plain English query. How many bones are there in the human body?

Quietly and efficiently, the search engine gets to work. Noisily and despairingly, Team A wallows in an overview of the life and times of Herophilus of Chalcedon, founder of modern anatomy. Quick! B for Bones! Over at the computer, a slack-jawed Team B contemplates the first in a batch of 20 809 483 responses. Something wrong here.

One half of the links are about Leonardo da Vinci, the rest are about nudism. Team B re-formats, instructing Infoseek to limit its search to all sites containing the exact phrase, 'bones in the human body'. But it's too late.

Team A hefts volume II of *Britannica* into the air and yells the answer in triumph: '206!' It will be at least another three seconds before Team B, now sifting through a field of 50 finely focused responses, is able to echo the factoid on the Health Trivia page of the St Francis Hospital in Topeka, Kansas. 206. We knew that.

All right, then. Who's the president of Ecuador? Good work, Team A. Unfortunately, the answer in the *World Almanac Book of Facts* is two years out of date. Wired to the Web, a smugly smiling Team B extracts the correct answer from the archive of recent news stories on the CNN site. Hey! Put that encyclopaedia down! It's only a game.

But in today's multimedia world, it's a game that proves a powerful point. No single source of information is all-encompassing and infallible. If you know what you're looking for, and where and how to find it, you can rest assured that the answer is somewhere out there on the Internet, in more depth and detail than you'll ever need.

But is the Internet quicker? Is it more efficient? Ask any bleary-eyed Internet addict who has ever logged on to confirm a simple fact — 'I just want to make sure of the correct spelling of Nelson Mandela's middle name' — only to come crashing down to earth after several hours adrift in the tangled web of hyperspace.

Yes, the Internet, like no other medium in history, has the power to expand minds, stimulate curiosity and build bridges between people.

But when last did you come across a librarian who said: 'DNS lookup failure. Server down. Please try again later', when you tabled a request for information?

Today's kids are lucky enough to live in an age that allows them to embrace all media and technologies in the pursuit of knowledge. A switched-on scholar with Internet access and a Shakespeare assignment can spend a few hushed hours in the public library, or he can surf on over to http://the-tech.mit.edu/Shakespeare/ works.html and glean everything he needs from a searchable database on a computer across the Atlantic.

Which doesn't mean he'll hand in a better assignment, or even hand it in on time. Information is just a currency. Its real value lies in how you spend it.

The Ebola assignment:
a case study in the art of sifting signal from noise

Your kid comes home from school one day with the kind of question parents dread the most: 'Mom, Dad, what do you know about Ebola?' Not much. You know it's somewhere out there. You know it's a virus. Other than that, your knowledge is limited to one indisputable fact: Everything you need to know about Ebola will be on the Internet.

You grab a notebook, check that the printer is loaded, and pull up a chair next to your kid. This is going to be what the educators like to call a 'collaborative learning experience'. The assignment: Trace the history and pattern of Ebola epidemics in Africa against a background of worldwide concern over new and emerging viruses.

It's a broad topic, but that's not the challenge. The challenge, as your co-researcher hastens to inform you, is that the teacher who handed out the assignment is an unusually switched-on and well-connected person. A teacher with Internet access. The warning has already been sounded: 'cut-and-paste' jobs will not be accepted.

Yes, use the Net by all means. But don't just regurgitate reams of information. First, find the *right* information. Then analyse it, interpret it, question it, dig beneath the surface of the facts to get at the truth. That's the challenge.

It's the art, as they say on the Internet, of sifting signal from noise — of surfing through channels of static and interference, until you find clarity and meaning.

The Internet's ease of access can be deceptive. You actually have to work harder and think smarter to make any sense of what you'll find out there. Go to a public library, ask for information on the Ebola virus, and you'll be presented with a handful of books, a couple of encyclopaedia references, and perhaps a selection of newspaper and magazine clippings. The information will already have been filtered to your requirements.

But on the Net ... well, let's be brave. Begin with an aerial view of the situation. Go to Dogpile (http://www.dogpile.com), a search engine that searches 23 other search engines and thousands of Usenet newsgroups to bring you more information, facts and opinions than you're ever going to need. Let's type in: Ebola. By using the pull-down menus, we'll instruct Dogpile to search the Web, followed by Usenet. Fetch!

Now for the hard work: filtering and weeding our way through the mass of responses. Search engines, as we've already learned, rank results in order of relevance. But they're not human. They're incapable of judging the value, veracity, credibility and accuracy of the information they so speedily present.

For instance, right up here in the first batch of results, we have two links to Ebola research papers posted by high school students who are no doubt proud of their work. But their papers turn out to be sketchy, melodramatic and conspicuously unreferenced. It's not hard to see why. These are Internet cut-and-paste jobs. To use them as sources would be to feed on information that has already been through the spin-dryer a couple of times.

We can also safely ignore the myriad of sites that offer the following thesis on Ebola: It's a 'cool' virus. On the Internet, any organism capable of turning your insides to soup is bound to wind up with its own fan club. So we have a page that puts Ebola on a par with the actor Leonardo DiCaprio on a listing of 'things that I love'. Then again, it pays not to make blanket judgements.

A separate link leads us to the 'Ebola Zaïre Fan Club', which turns out to a mine of useful information, putting a colloquial, tongue-in-cheek spin on the virus while linking us to the professional and academic sites that will best serve our needs. These would include the home pages of the Centres for Disease Control (CDC) in Atlanta, the Department of Microbiology at the University of Cape Town, the Institute for Molecular Virology at the University of Wisconsin, and the excellent Outbreak site, with its solid scientific background and up-to-the-minute tracking of viral epidemics across the globe.

This is where the Internet begins to get the edge over even the most well-stocked public library. A click of the mouse gives us access to doctoral papers, news reports, press statements, interviews with experts, articles in medical and scientific journals, and in-depth discussions in online forums. But we still need to evaluate, we still need to filter. Frank Molinek, a senior librarian at the Davidson College in Charlotte, North Carlina, offers the following criteria for assessing the worth of a site for academic research:

⇢ What is the site's purpose?
⇢ Will the information be unbiased?
⇢ Who sponsors the site?

- What are the organisation's values or goals?
- Is the information well documented, with citations to sources used in obtaining the information?
- What are the author's credentials?
- How does the value of the Web-based information compare with other available sources, such as print?

As Davidson points out, it's mostly a matter of common sense. But in the online rush, when you're drowning in information, it's easy to lose sight of the rules. These should apply even more stringently when the quest takes you to the Net's free-for-all newsgroups.

A search for 'Ebola' on the Reference.com site (http://www.reference.com) will turn up dozens of hits from newsgroups and mailing lists. But the context could range from cult movies (alt.cult-movies) to computer gaming (alt.games.redalert) to the reading habits of disaffected 20-somethings (alt.society.generation-x).

Indeed, there is so much noise on the newsgroups, that they should be pursued only as a sideline, or when all other avenues of enquiry have been exhausted.

The upside is that you may be able to plunge straight into a debate or controversy on a specialist forum like bionet.virology, with the added prospect of direct e-mail communication with the participants. A personal interview with a professor of virology in Cape Town or Wisconsin will always add value to a school report.

Finally, don't forget the online editions of newspapers and magazines. Many allow you to search their archives, a privilege previously extended only to the ink-and-nicotine-stained fraternity of journalism. Now, with little or no danger of inhaling secondary tobacco smoke, or having to decipher yellowing clippings from bygone days — not for nothing is a newspaper library known as a 'morgue' — you can click your way through crisply presented news reports and features in the comfort of your own home.

A tip-off from the Ebola Zaïre Fan Club leads us to a series of award-winning articles in the *Nando Times*, lending a sense of drama and immediacy to our growing stockpile of academic dissertations.

Closer to home, we raid the archives of the *Mail & Guardian* (http://wn.apc.org/wmail/issues/) as well as the *Independent Online* (http://www.inc.co.za) for local backgrounders, profiles and insights.

Once again, a healthy dose of scepticism is called for. Newspapers are only as reliable as their own sources, and increasingly, those sources are to be found on the Internet itself. It's easy to get caught in a whirlpool of misinformation, inaccuracies, and opinion masquerading as fact. Young researchers should be taught not to take information on the Internet at face value, but to trace it as far back as possible to its source.

For instance, an Ebola report in *The Star* may include a brief quote from Professor Bob Swanepoel of the National Institute for Virology. With a little bit of sifting on the Net, we can uncover the full text of the original press statement. If nothing else, such exercises will teach the researcher a great deal about the way news is sourced, filtered and put together.

For adults and children alike, the real value of the Internet is that it has brought democracy and — pardon my jargon — transparency to the process of gathering information. All that remains is to make that process work for you. Let's see. We've been online, desperately seeking Ebola, for two hours, 45 minutes and 26 seconds. The little meter in the corner of the screen gives us a reading of R16,80, local-call time. Not bad. Cheaper than photostatting books and encyclopaedias, anyway.

The hard copy has piled up on the desk. The printer has run out of paper. Magically cloning documents from computers across the world, we've extracted only a fraction of the available information on the subject. Now comes the greatest challenge of all. Doing our homework.

Ten top tips for surefire searching

1. Don't limit your search to the Web Wide as it may be, the Web represents only a fraction of the Internet's available information resources. Use Deja News (http://www.dejanews.com) to scan more than 18 000 Usenet newsgroups for inside info on any subject under, above and beyond the sun. There are too many subjects, in fact. Parental guidance is strongly advised. But a Usenet search, used the right way, can provide fascinating insights into otherwise tired topics, with the added prospect of instant e-mail connections to experts in the field.

2. Don't stray from the path A simple search can take forever if you follow every random hyperlink to its logical conclusion. Better to bookmark interesting byways, and return to them at your leisure.

3. Use the news If you're searching for up-to-the-minute information on topical subjects, look beyond the big search engines, and explore the in-house archives of the world's great newspapers and magazines. You'll find a huge list on Ecola's Newsstand (http://www.ecola.com).

4. Don't just search — MetaSearch MetaSearch engines are search engines that search other search engines to maximise your information returns. They can be too much of a good thing, not to mention too much of a slow thing, but they're good starting-points if you're interested in looking at the big picture. Try the inelegantly named but very powerful Dogpile (http://www.dogpile.com) for starters.

5. Separate the wheat from the chaff Whether they return dozens, hundreds or millions of links, most search engines sort their results in order of relevancy. If you don't find what you're looking for in the first 10 or 20 links, forget the rest, and rephrase your query.

6. Use the Find button on your browser Sometimes it's a little difficult to work out why a search turned up a particular document. That's because the search term you're looking for may be right at the bottom of the page. Use Find (under the Edit menu in Internet Explorer and Netscape) to hunt them down in a hurry.

7. Use wildcards Most search engines allow you to use wildcard characters — such as *, #, or ? — to broaden your search when you're not sure of spelling or usage. Searching for 'Be*tles', for instance, will lead you to the pop group as well as the insect, not to mention the VW bug.

8. Search beyond words As the Web's biggest, brightest search engines go out of their way to outdo each other, many now offer instant access to multimedia files, including sound clips and clipart. Great for school projects. Try Yahoo's Image Surfer (http://ipix.yahoo.com/isurf.html) or Lycos Pictures & Sounds Directory (http://www.lycos.com/lycos-media.html).

9. Save your searches It's a good idea to hold on to particularly fruitful searches for future reference. Bookmark the results, and don't forget to hit the Search button again to update the search.

10. **Know when to stop** So much information, so many search engines, so little time. Even when you're sure you've found what you're looking for, the temptation to carry on searching can be hard to resist. But try, or you could be lost in the black hole of cyberspace forever.

When in doubt, ask an expert

Despite the terrible things people say about the Internet, it remains a place with an almost Utopian sense of community. No matter what you need to know, or how obscure your field of interest, there'll always be someone who is willing to help, expecting nothing in return but world fame and the warm glow that comes from doing good.

These are the experts of the Internet, an ever-widening web of academics, specialists, hobbyists, professionals and field workers who have volunteered their virtual services in the cause of spreading knowledge and enlightenment about their chosen disciplines. Visit their Web sites, study their credentials, peruse their opinions and papers. And if there's anything else you need to know, just ask.

But first…

Many 'Ask the Expert' sites feature lists of frequently asked questions (FAQs). It's good manners to peruse the list before firing away in case your question has already been answered.

➠ Experts are busy people. Don't clog up their mailboxes with complicated multi-part questions or queries outside their field of expertise.
➠ Bearing workloads and time zones in mind, allow at least three days for an answer, although you may get one sooner if your question is unusually interesting or thought-provoking.
➠ As willing as they are to help, experts don't do homework. Not other people's, anyway.
➠ Include your name, age and country of origin with your question.

Now fire away.

Ask an Antarctic Expert
WWW address:
http://icair.iac.org.nz/~psommerv/web/askaques/askaques.htm
Are there any yellow-eyed penguins in Antarctica? Why does it snow even in summer? How does the ceiling manage to stay up in an igloo?

All the facts from the frozen wastes, courtesy of people who have actually been there.

Ask an English grammar expert
WWW address: http://www.lydbury.co.uk/grammar/index.html
The place, as it were, to find out once and for all why we don't say 'as it was'.

Ask Dr Math
WWW address: http://forum.swarthmore.edu/dr.math/
Er, shouldn't that be 'Dr Maths'? Never mind. Whatever your language or level of confusion, the doc will apply his mind to your most mind-numbing mathematical conundrums. But watch out — he's just as likely to throw one your way in return.

Ask an astronaut
WWW address: http://www.nss.org/askastro/form.html
Spacewalkers, moonleapers, shuttlebugs and lady spacepersons. An out-of-this-world chance to ask them anything you want to know. But please — not the one about how they go to the bathroom in outer space.

Ask a genetic scientist
WWW address: http://www.ag.auburn.edu/~mwooten/form1.html
Dr Michael Wooten is Associate Professor of Genetics at Auburn University, USA. His special interests are 'beach mice, mosquitofish, and other non-human vertebrates', but he'll be happy to answer general questions on issues at the forefront of genetic science. Go on — ask him how long it will be before you're able to clone yourself.

Ask a Bible specialist
WWW address: http://www.bibleinfo.com/question.html
From Genesis to Revelations, if it's in the Bible and you don't understand it, apply here for enlightenment.

Ask a zookeeper
WWW address: http://www.imon.com/mgzoo/pages/ask.htm
It's a long way from the bushveld to Lodi, California, so don't forget to ask if the lions are feeling homesick.

Ask a kid
WWW address: http://plaza.interport.net/kids_space/mail/bulletin/questions.html
This is where kids from around the world meet to ask each other the kind of questions their parents kept asking when they were kids.

Ask a bug expert
WWW address: http://www.orkin.com/bugdoctor.html
You may not want them in your home, or at least not in your hair, but insects play a very important role in our ecosystem. Just ask the entomologist (and if you don't know what that means, ask the bug expert).

Ask a dinosaur expert
WWW address: http://denr1.igis.uiuc.edu/isgsroot/dinos/rjjinput_form.html
Fresh from the fossil grounds of Hell Creek, South Dakota, Dino Russ will be pleased to fill you in on hadrosaurs, tyrannosaurs, pachycephalosaurs, dromeosaurs and any other saurs you dare to mention.

Ask the Amish
WWW address: http://www.800padutch.com/askamish.html
While they frown on electricity and other frivolities of the modern world, this cloistered community in Dutch Pennsylvania has taken a giant leap into cyberspace as part of a campaign to increase tolerance and understanding. Sample question: 'Why do you guys grow beards without moustaches?'

Ask an astronomer
WWW address: http://www2.ari.net/home/odenwald/qadir/qanda.html
Instead of staring at the sky all night, step inside and ask Dr Sten Odenwald to tell you what you're staring at.

Ask a veterinarian
WWW address: http://www.pawprints.com/VETCONNECT/askthevet.html
His surgery is all the way in Canada, but you're welcome to quizz him on your pet subject.

Ask a volcanologist
WWW address: http://volcano.und.nodak.edu/vwdocs/ask_a.html
Volcanology assignment looming and you can't find a decent volcano anywhere in the country? Don't blow your top. Just fire away.

Ask a mad scientist
WWW address: http://128.252.223.239/~ysp/MSN/
'Why, and how, does a rubber ball bounce, as opposed to a cement ball?' No wonder scientists go mad, having to answer questions like this.

Ask a cryptography expert
WWW address: http://www.fatmans.demon.co.uk/crypt/index.htm
Bzm xnt qdzc sghr? Is so; you must be a cryptography expert yourself. All the inside info on the art and science of secret writing.

Ask a tropical fish expert
WWW address: http://www.kiva.net/~robert/fish/fish_help.html
Are zebrafish black with white stripes, or ... hey, ask someone who knows.

Ask a bubbles expert
WWW address: http://bubbles.org/pbfa2.htm
If there's anything you absolutely need to know about the art of blowing the perfect bubble, pop the question to Professor Bubbles (not his real name).

Ask a gravity expert
WWW address:
http://www.physics.umd.edu/rgroups/gen_rel_the/question.html
Is there gravity in cyberspace? The expert awaits your even weightier questions.

Ask a classical musician
WWW address: http://www.smcm.edu/~dfroom/
His name is David Froom, he's Associate Professor of Music at St Mary's College in Maryland, and he performs his own classical compositions to great acclaim in his spare time. Ask him anything you want, as long as it's classical.

Help yourself to the world's ultimate homework helper

I was looking for a suitable quotation about information to kick off this chapter. I could have spun around in my chair, whipped *The Oxford Dictionary of Quotations* from the shelf, and tracked down another timeless gem from Dr Samuel Johnson in a minute or so.

But 222 years had flown by since the doctor last discussed the dual nature of knowledge with his good friend Boswell, and I was too busy staring at a computer screen to flip through the pages of a dusty reference tome. Fortunately, I had done my homework. I dialled into the World Wide Web, and connected to a site that has become one of my favourite sources of useful information on the Internet: B.J. Pinchbeck's Homework Helper, at http://tristate.pgh.net/~pinch13/

B.J. Pinchbeck is nine years old. He lives in a suburb of Pennsylvania, USA, where his buddies call him 'Beege', and the teachers insist on calling him 'Bruce, Jr'. His claim to fame? Helping kids and grown-ups do their homework.

Samuel Johnson said: 'We know a subject ourselves, or we know where we can find information upon it.' B.J. Pinchbeck says: 'If you can't find it here, then you just can't find it.' He's probably right.

In a no-frills, user-friendly style that has earned his site dozens of awards, B.J. provides tried-and-tested links to more than 350 helpful sites in ten categories of interest.

Looking for the latest in medical and pharmaceutical research? Looking for pictures of bugs, slugs and other creepy-crawlies? Looking for the full text of a classic book that you just can't find on your shelves? Looking for an elusive quotation by Dr Samuel Johnson? Look no further.

B.J.'s site is a one-stop information station that is mind-boggling in its scope, yet simple enough to be of practical use to even the youngest of Web surfers. It is also, as it turns out, an excellent example of a parent and child joining forces to get the best out of the Net, and providing a helpful service to other users in return.

B.J.'s father, Bruce Pinchbeck, is a computer specialist and trainer whose main field of interest is the use of computers in medical social work. He introduced B.J. — 'a wonderful boy with a neat sense of humour' — to the wonders of the Internet in 1996 and, although the computer-crazy youngster had little difficulty finding his way around, he was initially overwhelmed by the sheer scale of the enterprise.

'The Net is a very big place,' said B.J. in an e-mail interview. 'It can be difficult to find the information you're looking for. As me and my dad surfed the Net, we kept thinking it would be a cool idea if we could put all the great educational sites we found on one page, so people wouldn't have to hunt all over for them.'

Father and son downloaded a shareware HTML editor from the Web (see the next chapter: How to make yourself a home on the World Wide Web) and, in one weekend, B.J. Pinchbeck's Homework Helper was up and running. I asked Bruce how the site had helped B.J. with his homework and school career.

'First of all, it's helped him develop an interest in a wide variety of subjects. It's amazing to hear some of the things he's learned. It's also helped him with specific school projects — not just because he knows how to find information, but because he knows how to find ideas.'

Still, Bruce warns that the Net should not be seen as a substitute for other avenues of learning. B.J. spends an average of four hours a week online, but he remains a regular visitor to the public library's reading room.

'The Internet has a way of capturing the imagination of young users,' says Bruce. 'There's no doubt that B.J.'s knowledge, as well as his views of the world, have changed very positively as a result of his experiences online. But you have to look at the Internet as one additional way to research information. It shouldn't become a replacement for more traditional resources.'

In the online world, B.J. Pinchbeck's Homework Helper will continue to grow, serving as an ever-expanding gateway to knowledge for other parents and children, and earning its young curator celebrity status that reaches far beyond his schoolroom in New Brighton, Pennsylvania. For B.J. and his father, this isn't just a home page on the information highway. This is home.

'Working on our site has helped to solidify our father–son relationship,' says Bruce. 'It's also given B.J. confidence in a lot of other areas. There's more to this than just helping my son with his homework. Establishing a home page, I believe, is one of the few areas of your life you can have some control over.'

Ready? Now it's your turn.

Chapter 14

A home on the Web

Build a place in cyberspace

Andy Warhol would have flipped his wig for the World Wide Web. Remember? He was the guy who predicted that everybody in the world would one day be famous for 15 minutes.

But even Andy, whose odd habits included taking a Polaroid photograph of every person he met, just in case they one day turned out to be famous, could hardly have envisioned a medium as conducive to instant celebrity as the Internet.

Whether you're a rocket scientist studying anti-matter in Antarctica, a rock guitarist raising hell in Helsinki, a needlework enthusiast with two kids in New Jersey, or a ten-year-old *X-Files* fan with a pet snake in Pofadder, this is where you go to tell the world about it.

You don't need a printing press, you don't need a TV station, you don't need a public relations consultant. All you need is a home page.

Strictly speaking, a home page is the opening or 'index' page of any site on the World Wide Web. Hence, you'll hear people talking about the IBM home page, the Disney home page, the White House home page. But as more and more home users go online, the term has come to refer to any page or site designed for personal, rather than corporate or professional use.

You can use a home page to tell the story of your life, vent your opinions, showcase your previously unpublished poetry, advertise your home baking business, and display your three-year-old's latest masterpiece of refrigerator art for all the world to see.

Indeed, your three-year-old can even have a home page of her own. Would that make her the youngest person in cyberspace? Forget it. Aside from all the bouncing babes and newborns with their own WWW addresses, the latest trend among the Wired Generation is to upload ultrasound scans of their budding offspring-to-be.

Here, as elsewhere on the Internet, there are no rules, no restrictions, no barriers to entry. Anyone with the right combination of hardware, software and self-confidence can build a home on the Web. Building a home anyone else would want to visit, on the other hand, takes a little more practice.

Teen movie critic and the koala kid: why they're so famous in cyberspace

I am completely redoing my page because it pretty much sucked. I have become educated enough about the Web to know that you don't care about who I am or where I live or how old I am. But maybe you want to hear about me. Maybe you are weird. So. I am 15 years old and I live in Cullowhee, NC. I don't have a scanner so you don't get to see a picture of me. In fact, why the hell do I have a page?
CLAIRE'S HOME PAGE, SOMEWHERE ON THE INFORMATION HIGHWAY

I've been to Canada and Japan, Alaska and Peru, Belgium, Bangkok and Benoni. I've wandered the slip-roads, side-routes and byways. I've met people of all ages, from every walk of life. I've learned what they like, dislike, look like. I've ventured into the abyss of human vanity and inconsequence. I've seen the personal home pages of the World Wide Web.

Pages and pages about people and their hobbies, people and their pets, people and the places they've been to on the Net. I'm exhausted. But I'm not complaining. For the truth is there are few greater pleasures on the Web than the serendipitous discovery of a well-designed, well-thought-out personal home page that has something of value to offer the casual surfer-by.

Maybe it's a page of lovingly curated links to little-known places of interest. Maybe it's a glimpse of everyday life in a faraway part of the world. Maybe it's a touch of offbeat humour, a heartfelt tale of survival, or a telling insight into teenage existentialism in Cullowhee, NC.

Whatever it is, if it draws your attention amidst a myriad of rival attractions, it will have achieved a distinction worth striving for in your own little corner of cyberspace. You don't need an excuse. You don't need a scanner.

All you need is an angle. Something that makes you, and your page, stand out from the pack. Enter Roger Davidson of California, USA. Bespectacled, computer-crazy and mad about the movies, Roger was

16 when he set out to build his first home page. Not to tell people about himself, but about his passion. His angle: Teen Movie Critic.

There are thousands of amateur and professional movie critics on the Web. But as Roger puts it: 'They're mostly adults. I thought it might be a good idea to do a film critic page from a young person's perspective.' The result was a smash hit. Teen Movie Critic (http://www.dreamagic.com/roger/teencritic1.html) is one of the Web's most visited and argued-about film sites. Roger's reviews of current and classic movies are short, sharp, often controversial.

Like almost anyone else with a home page, he's merely venting his opinions. But that angle — that young person's perspective — has been enough to earn him fame and a certain notoriety on the world's most crowded public forum. I asked Roger how having a home page on the Web had made a difference to his life.

'I've learned how to communicate better with people. I've also learned that the Internet can be a perfect creative outlet for people like me, who feel they aren't being heard enough or that their talents aren't being noticed. Now a whole generation, that was once silenced, can speak freely and show their talents and skills to the world.'

But it's not just teens who are taking up the challenge. Let's click across to Karana Downs, on the Brisbane River in Queensland, Australia. Home of Alexander Scott Balson. Artist, entrepreneur, Web page designer. Well, all right — he gets a little help from his dad. For Alex, as his fans around the world will tell you, is only six years old.

Alex's angle, on the home page that bears his name, is koalas. In particular, a trouble-prone koala known as Max. Koala Trouble (http://www.peg.apc.org/~balson/story/bookmain.html) is a series of interactive escapades in which Max gets into and out of mischief with his fellow marsupials. The stories are not huge on plot — Max sees kangaroo in water; kangaroo calls for help; Max throws kangaroo a branch; kangaroo hops to safety — but their charm and simplicity have generated more than hundreds of 'hits' and thousands of e-mail messages since the site made its début in 1996.

Only the year before, Alex had been introduced to the wonders of the Web by his father Scott, a professional Web designer. It was not a case of love at first site.

'I spent a few hours surfing the Net, and bookmarked a selection of sites aimed at young kids. I sat Alex down in front of the computer. After a few minutes of looking at reams of text and slow-loading pictures, he said, "Dad, this is boring," and walked off.'

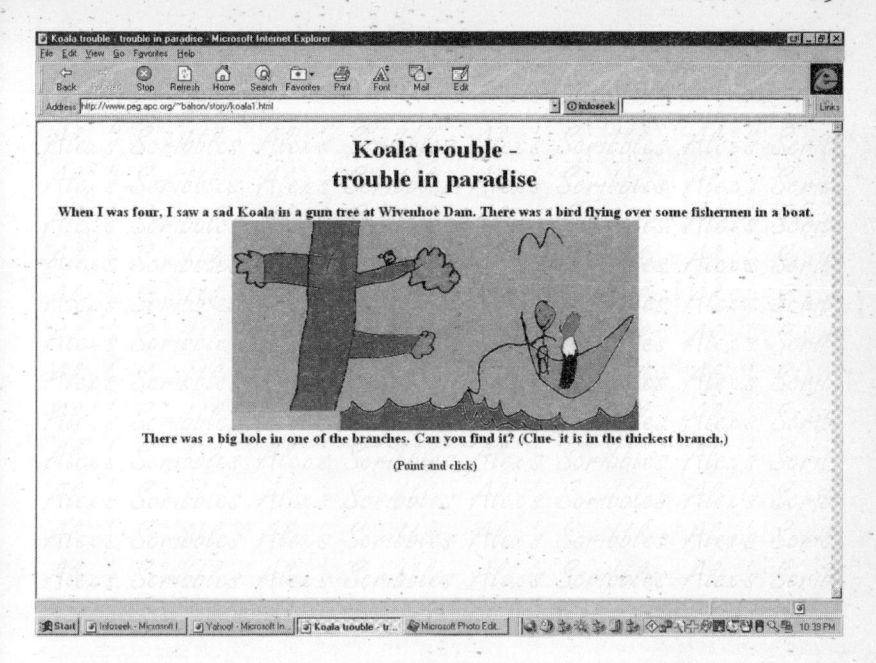

The turning point came when Scott saw Alex drawing an outline of a koala, inspired by a sighting of a marsupial in the wild, and his own fluffy toy with cork-ringed hat. 'I sat down next to Alex and said, "Why don't we do a little story about your koala?" First, we had to find a name. Max seemed pretty good.'

Before long that little story — 'Help Max Find His Mummy' — found its way on to the Web, along with pictures drawn by Alex and scanned into the computer by Dad. Today, Alex is a Net celebrity, proud winner of the under-15 category of Australia's biggest Internet award. But the stories have brought him more than fame and acclaim.

They've sown the seeds of a business empire. Alex's scribbles have all the hallmarks — broad, jagged outlines and bold splashes of colour — of art generated by a mouse on a computer screen. But they look great on T-shirts. And mouse-pads. And coffee mugs and tablecloths and bedspreads. Who knows? There might even be a movie in this. At the very least, an animated series.

For Alexander Balson, co-founder and director of Alex's scribbles, the Net profits are rolling in. Says Dad: 'There is no other form of media in the world where someone so young, with so little resources, can launch a successful global merchandising business. At six years old, Alex is learning to use the Internet not only as a powerful tool for gathering information, but as a hands-on educational vehicle for building and running a business in the world of computer networks.'

But the lesson here is not how to make a million on the Web. It's how to turn an everyday interest or activity — going to the movies, drawing pictures, making up silly stories for your kid — into an enterprise that captures the imagination of an online community.

The word 'enterprise' is not used loosely here. Commercial spin-offs may be a rarity for a humble home page, but the best and most successful sites will always be those that trade in the real currency of the Internet. Not money, but ideas. No matter how crowded the Net may get, there'll always be room for a fresh perspective, a new spin, an original angle. And once again, it doesn't have to be anything of earth-shattering consequence.

Jackson's Page for Five Year Olds (http://www.islandnet.com/~bedford/jackson.html) is just that — a page of links to interesting places for five-year-olds. Graphically, it's nothing to e-mail home about and, even for its target audience, it seems a little slim on content (Power Rangers, Lego, moon rockets, hamsters). But the site has been showered with acclaim by the many arbiters of excellence on the Net, and it isn't hard to see why. In biz-speak, Jackson's Page adds value to the Internet by offering a personalised service to a focused niche market. The possibilities are endless. One day, Jackson will be six. A whole new franchise will be born.

Also point your browser at Maddy Mayhem's 100% Fun! Page (http://wchat.on.ca/merlene/kid.htm). Can anybody resist a kids' page based on that promise? Especially when Maddy — real name Madelin — lives up to her promise and her nickname on a site that whirls through the world of a typical seven-year-old. With a little help from Mom, Maddy celebrates reading and friendship, recipes and riddles, and reviews the latest movies with an exclamation-marked exuberance that puts even Teen Movie Critic to shame.

Sites like these stand out not because of what they offer, but because of the way they connect. They're alive with enthusiasm, for the Internet and the world outside. You want to pay these sites the ultimate compliment: They're bookmarkable. But they're only the beginning.

If you're planning to build a home page with, for or about your kids, you need look no further for an angle than your own home, your own home town, your own Rainbow Nation. Here are some possibilities:

- a three-year-old's What I did at Kindergarten Today Page
- a six-year-old's Wild Beasts of the South African Jungle Page
- an eight-year-old VidKid's TV and Video Review Page
- a nine-year-old's Everything You Wanted to Know about Nelson Mandela Page
- an 11-year-old Entymologist's Parktown Prawn Appreciation Page
- a young Johannesburger's Max the Gorilla Fan Club Page
- a teenager's eye-view of Crime and Violence in Gauteng
- a 17-year-old's My Life in Soweto Page.

Got it? Now let's move on to the technical stuff.

How to <SPEAK> HTML

What does a personal home page look like? That's entirely up to you. It can be a bare-bones block of text with rudimentary graphics, or a mind-blowing multimedia extravaganza with MIDI sound and animated images. It can be a single, scroll-down page with no external links, or a multiple-page site that could keep you surfing for days.

Either way, your primary construction tool will be a programming language called HTML: Hypertext Markup Language. If you think that sounds scary, wait till you see what it looks like:

<HTML><HEAD><TITLE>Meet Chantessy</TITLE></HEAD>
<BODY BACKGROUND="b-newyr.gif"><CENTER>
<IMG SRC="l-pstars.gif">
<IMG SRC="chanti.gif"ALT="Picture of Chantessy">
<IMG SRC="l-pstars.gif">
Hi! My name is Chantessy. I'm ten years old and live in California.
I like to read, write, do arts and crafts, and explore the Internet!

<HR SIZE = 6>

Relax. Programming in HTML is just as easy as writing in English. (Ha!) The secret lies in the syntax: Those cryptic codes between angle brackets are nothing more or less than the building-blocks of the World Wide Web.

They're called 'tags', and what they do is instruct your Web browser to display text or images in the format of your choice. Tags work wonders. If you were looking at Chantessy's home page right now, for instance, you'd see that ugly clump of coding transformed into a picture of Chantessy, bidding you welcome against a background of balloons and streamers.

The words 'Meet Chantessy' would appear in the title bar at the top of your browser. Rows of pink stars would frame Chantessy's portrait, and her short-and-sweet greeting would be centred, justified and displayed in bold type.

See? Even a ten-year-old can program in HTML. But if there isn't one around, you're probably going to need a little professional help. To start with, I recommend you head straight for the following site: http://junior.apk.net/*jbarta/tutor/makapage/index.html. There you will find a friendly Web wizard named Joe Barta who will show you the ropes in six easy online lessons.

Barta is a professional Web designer, and his witty tutorial — *So You Want to Make a Web Page!* — promises to turn even the klutziest computer user into an amateur Web designer within five minutes. If you're not in such a rush, you can also try out one of the many shareware and commercial HTML editing programs on the market.

These programs range from the free and friendly WebThing (http://www.arachnoid.com/lutusp/webthing.htm) to the ultracool *HotDog Pro* (http://www.sausage.com) to the powerful and expensive *HotMetaL Pro* (available at your neighbourhood computer hyper). While these packages can make your life easier by memorising complex HTML tags, importing and converting text, and providing templates for awesome, industrial-strength Web pages, they can just as easily overwhelm the novice user and slow down what is essentially a straightforward editing process.

For now, all you need is a plain-text editor, such as Notepad (free with any version of Windows), and one major technical skill: the ability to locate the '< >' keys on your keyboard. Found them yet? Good. Let's make a home page.

My very first home page

A home page on the Web is really no more than an HTML file, and an HTML file is really no more than a plain-text file with an '.htm' extension. So, first thing we do, we open up Notepad and create a new file, which we will call homepage.htm. Actually, sorry — first thing we do is create a new directory called HTML, because that's where we'll be storing all the .htm, text and image files that will eventually be sent to their new home in cyberspace.

This is a process called 'uploading', which we'll worry about later. Now let's type something in that vast expanse of blank space.

<HTML>

That's right — it's a tag. Tags can be in upper or lowercase, but big letters are better for OBVIOUS REASONS. There are dozens of tags in the HTML vocabulary, but we need not concern ourselves with more than a handful at this stage. The thing to remember is that HTML tags, like Grey Loeries, tend to hang around in pairs. The first tag will 'switch on' a format or style, while the second will switch it off. Like so:

<HTML></HTML>
<HEAD></HEAD>
<TITLE></TITLE>
<BODY></BODY>

As you'll notice, it's the little '/' that makes all the difference — the off-switch. Forgetting to switch off a tag on a Web page is almost as dangerous as forgetting to switch off the stove when you've just finished making chips. You really don't want to see what happens. Now let's go back and give our home page a title:

<HTML>
<HEAD>
<TITLE>Sarah Jane's Absolutely Loony Lion King Page</TITLE>
</HEAD>

The title will appear in the thin bar at the very top of your Web browser, as well as in the bookmark file of anyone who is kind enough to bookmark your page. So make sure you choose something catchy, descriptive and relevant. Now let's move on to the interesting stuff.

```
<BODY BACKGROUND="simba.gif">
<CENTER>
<H1>The Lion King</H1>
<H3><I>If You're Absolutely Loony About The Lion King, You've Come to the Right Place!</I></H3>
<HR>
</CENTER>
<CENTER>
<IMG WIDTH=420 HEIGHT=100 SRC="lionking.gif">
<BGSOUND SRC="hakuna.mi"'>
</CENTER>
```

Translation? The BODY BACKGROUND is the wallpaper of our home page. A subtle yet unmistakable outline of the young Simba that we, um, appropriated from somebody else's home page. It's incredibly easy to do this. If you come across an image, graphic or photograph you like, click your right mouse button on it and save it to your HTML directory for later use. (With reservations — see the cautionary note on plagiarism in 'Tips for a top home page' on page 161.)

Next up, we have a centred, bold-type heading to our home page. *(Note:* The wrong spelling of <CENTER> is the right spelling.) For our header format, we can choose from six levels in declining sizes, beginning with the easy-on-the-eye <H1>. For our subhead, we choose an <H3> heading, in italics *for added emphasis.*

The <HR>, a rare partnerless tag, gives us a neat horizontal line across the page, which leads into a modestly sized picture of the cast of *The Lion King.* And the <BGSOUND> tag? That instructs the browser to play a background sound file, in this case a digitised instrumental version of *Hakuna Matata,* which will be heard in its full glory by anyone with a sound card in their computer. Wow! It's just like TV! Now it's time to say hello to the world:

```
<P>
```
Hakuna matata, everybody! Hello and welcome to my Absolutely Loony Lion King Page. My name is Sarah Jane. I'm three-and-a-half years old, and I stay in <A HREF="http://www.marques.co.za/"> South Africa.</A><P>

My favourite things are music, painting, <A HREF="http://members.aol.com/belledoll/internetbarbieclub.html">Barbie</A>, books, computers, and <A HREF="http://www.dinosaurmall.com/">dinosaurs</A>. But the thing I'm most absolutely loony about is The Lion King.<P>
Do you know how many times I've seen it? Forty-two-and-a-half! The half-a-time was when the videotape broke, and my dad had to rush out and buy a new one.
<P>
<HR>

The <P>s are easy. All they do is format the text into paragraphs. But the <A></A>s represent HTML at its most arcane and powerful. They're called 'anchor tags', and they're the secret behind the true magic of the Web: hyperlinking. The HREF after the opening <A> stands for 'hypertext reference', which is the Web address you see in inverted commas after the = sign.

Any text between the anchor tags is automagically linked to that address, and will appear underlined and highlighted, usually in blue, on our Web page. Clicking on the Barbie link, for instance, will take the reader directly to The Internet Barbie Fan Club. You can never have too many links on a home page. Actually, you can. So let's limit ourselves to just a few more:

<H3>Try My favourite Loony Lion King Links!</H3>
<UL>
<LI><A HREF="http://www.disney.com">The Official Disney Lion King Page</A>
<LI><A HREF="http://www.lionking.org/scripts/">The full Lion King script</A>
<LI><A HREF="http://www.lionking.org/lyrics/">All The Lion King Song Lyrics</A>
<LI><A HREF="http://the-tech.mit.edu/Shakespeare">Shakespeare's Hamlet</A> (Has anyone noticed that this guy copied his plot from The Lion King? What a cheek!)
</UL>

What we have here, aside from the links, is a simple list in bullet-point form. The <BR> at the end of each link gives us a line break, while the </UL> remembers to switch the list format off. Well, that's our home page. It's a basic model, and it won't win any awards, but it's a solid foundation for our future in cyberspace. We can add to it, build on it, renovate, redesign, and totally change our minds. It's home. Which leaves us with just one little detail to take care of…

<HR>
Thanks for visiting my home page! You can e-mail me at <A HREF="mailto:loony@netcon.co.za">loony@netcon.co.za</A>
That's my dad's address, 'cos I can't read yet.
<HR>
</BODY>
</HTML>

By clicking on the address inside those tags, a visitor to your page will conjure up a handy e-mail message form, with your address already filled in. Impressed? You ain't seen nothing yet. Master HTML's staggering arsenal of tricks, and you can build a home page with tables, forms, frames, animations and text that changes colour, fades in and out, and scrolls across your screen like a tickertape. Oh yes, and don't forget this one:

<BLINK>Hello! Welcome to my blinking home page!</BLINK>

Now forget it. Any Web page that reminds you of your video recorder after a power failure, is to be avoided at all costs. The same goes for most HTML 'special effects'. Wonderful as they may seem, they tend to defeat the single most important reason why anybody would want to visit your home page. And that is to look at the content.

Moving in (and keeping house)
A home page is your own patch of turf in the fastest-growing, most colourful neighbourhood of the Electronic Global Village. But the really good news is that you won't need to take out a second mortgage.

If you're a dial-up subscriber to an Internet service — the likeliest scenario for a home user — you should be entitled to as much as two megabytes of 'virtual real estate' on the company's Web server. That's more than enough to host a home page. If your Internet service provider expects you to pay extra for the privilege, complain bitterly and trek to Geocities (http://www.geocities.com).

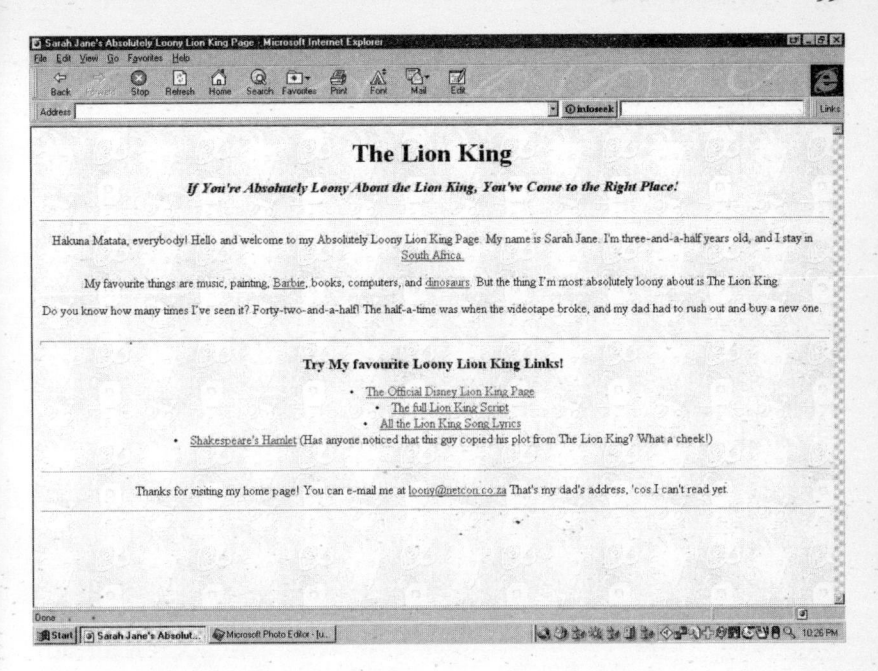

This is an excellent US-based service that offers free home pages in a variety of theme-based neighbourhoods, from SunsetStrip (for late-night jollers) to HotSprings (for health and fitness nuts) to Enchanted Forest (for cybertots and pre-teens). Even if you don't take up residence, stroll around Geocities for inspiration. You'll find some of the best-designed, most entertaining and informative home pages on the Web here.

Once you're satisfied that your home page is ready to be revealed to the world, you'll need to gather all your HTML, text, image and multimedia files in one place for uploading to your ISP's Web server. In plain English, you'll be transferring files to a remote computer, using a process known as FTP (File Transfer Protocol). For this you'll need a piece of software called an 'FTP client'. The one I like is CuteFTP, which you can download from http://www.cuteftp.com.

That's the hard part. The rest is as easy as:

1. Log on to your ISP's FTP site. (Ask your ISP for the address. It'll usually be something like mail.isp.co.za). You'll also have to enter your username and password to gain access to your private space on the server.
2. Once you're in, create a new directory according to your ISP's instructions.
3. Transfer your home page and all related files to the new directory. (Don't worry — the originals will remain on your own computer.)
4. Disconnect.
5. Go home.

The details vary from ISP to ISP, so you'll probably need to spend a few minutes on the helpline, or read the fine print on your ISP's home page. And what if you want to change, rearrange or update your site from time to time? An excellent idea. Simply edit the original files to your heart's content, and upload the pages as before.

Is that it? Not quite. Unless you're the shy and retiring type, you'll want to let the world know you've arrived, and are ready to receive visitors. You can make use of several 'Web Announcement' services, which will add your site to their 'What's New' listings, submit your details to the major search engines, or add your home page to their own mega-directories of interesting places to visit.

Some of these companies will want to charge you in US dollars for the service. Good luck to them. These are free:

- What's New Too (http://newtoo.manifest.com/WhatsNewToo/submit.html)
- InfoSpace (http://www.infospace.com/submit.html)
- NerdWorld (http://nerdworld.com).

If you believe your home page will be of interest to the users of a specific newsgroup, you can also post a short message containing the address and any other tantalising details. Most e-mail programs display a Web address as a hyperlink, allowing the reader to click and connect directly to the site.

We might wish to broadcast our Absolutely Loony Lion King Page on alt.fan.lion-king, alt.fan.disney, alt.kids.misc, alt.kids-talk, and alt.animals.felines.lions. Sending it to alt.disney.the-evil-empire, on the other hand, would not be such a good idea.

Tips for a top home page

Go straight to the source If you come across a home page you particularly admire, turn admiration into inspiration by cracking the code. Click on View and Source in your Web browser's menu, and you'll be presented with a raw HTML document that you can use as a 'cut-and-paste' model for your own home masterpiece.

Put it down on paper With links, text, graphics and images all over the place, the geography of a Web site can get confusing — even if it's your own. Before you lose your way, map out the site on a real page. Then get virtual.

Keep it simple The Web is full of battleship-grey pages with black text and blue hyperlinks, but at least you can read them. Not so for psychedelic backgrounds, scrolling banners, and blinking text in Day-Glo colours. There are more interesting ways to develop a migraine in this world.

Use small graphics Life is too short to watch a Web page load. The pictures on your home page may be fascinating and unique, but the Web's wide range of rival attractions severely limits the attention-spans of ... what were we saying again?

Double-check your links Few things are more infuriating to a Web surfer than a cul-de-sac on the information highway. Avoid those dreaded '404: Page Not Found' errors by regularly testing your links and updating them if necessary.

You don't have to tell people to 'Click here' any more The Web has been around long enough for the concept of hyperlinking to have sunk in a little. Even novice users can usually work out what to do when their travelling cursor turns into a pointing hand. *(Note for novice users: Click there.)*

Check spelling before uploading pages The Internet may be the acceptable face of anarchy in today's information society, but spelling still rools, OK? (Sorry. That should be 'roolz'.) Use the spellchecker in your word-processing program or HTML editor.

Borrow discreetly Although the culture of the Internet encourages the sharing of information and ideas, plagiarism is another kettle of somebody else's fish. It's a fine line and all that, but you can safely draw it at the lifting of words and images that have 'copyright' written all over them. Children, especially, should be taught what constitutes unacceptable borrowing in cyberspace.

Dump those cute construction signs A little constructive criticism: The most irritating thing on the Web just has to be that little graphic of the guy in the hard hat, alongside the disclaimer that 'This page is always under construction.' It's an unconvincing excuse for an unfinished page, and it's also redundant — everyone knows the entire Internet is always under construction. As, indeed, is the universe.

Keep the content alive The Web may not be as up-to-the-minute as radio or as immediate as television, but it remains a medium driven by freshness and novelty. Give visitors to your home page at least one good reason to bookmark and return.

Wow! Free stuff for your home page

Looking for icons, buttons, borders, backgrounds, clipart and other cool items to spruce up your home page? Look no further:

Doodle's Graphics Directory
WWW address:
http://www.geocities.com/SiliconValley/6603/index.html
These'll doodle nicely.

The Icon Depot
WWW address: artdzn.com/doodles/grafx/butns/butns.html
Mega-warehouse of icons for all seasons and reasons.

Stevie's Graphics, Pictures and Sounds
WWW address:
http://www.steview.com/cgi-bin/STEVIE/stev_graphics
Over 20 000 of them, also available in zipped format.

Yikes!
WWW address: http://members.aol.com/BEATFACY/index.html
As the name suggests, a wonderful archive of eye-boggling graphics.

And finally: HTML for cowards
Does HTML still look like $\delta\Sigma\Gamma\Lambda\Psi$ to you? Does the thought of programming anything more complicated than a pop-up toaster fill you with panic? Are you just too busy to even attempt to grasp the intricacies of a twelfth official language? You are not alone. Here are two ways to build a perfectly adequate home page without having to look an HTML tag in the face:

The Home Page Creation Centre
WWW address: http://the-inter.net/www/future21/create1.html
If you can fill in a job application form (albeit not for a job in home page design), you're already halfway on the road to your own home page. Just fill in the blanks at the centre's online site, and your barebones page will be coded and compressed for downloading in a matter of minutes.

The Web Wizard
WWW address: http://www.halcyon.com/artamedia/webwizard/.
This excellent little shareware program, available in Windows 3.1 and Windows 95 versions, will construct a home page to your specifications in eight easy steps. Naturally, the options are limited, but you do get a choice of background colours, a bullet-pointed list, and a selection of links to popular sites.

Part Four
Schools and Computers

Chapter 15

Goodbye, Mr Chips

Computers in the classroom

One fine day in the year 2025, our hero — let's call him Sipho — peeks through his bedroom window and decides to do something he hasn't done in ages. Go to school.

He taps a button on his WristTop computer and points it at the liquid-crystal screen on the wall. Great. There's an hour's worth of desk space up for grabs at the InterCity Educational Facility on the other side of town. Leaping out of bed, Sipho aims the WristTop at his face and sends a short v-mail to confirm he's on his way.

He can't believe his luck. Usually, homeschoolers have to book space at the EdFac weeks in advance. Grabbing an apple and a peanut-butter sandwich on the way out, Sipho shouts farewell to his parents and hops aboard a passing ElectroBus.

In minutes, the smokeless, driverless vehicle drops him outside a sprawling steel and glass complex, its central pyramid reflecting a rainbow of colours in the early-morning sunshine.

As he makes his way past trees, sportsfields and the ever-popular Edutainment Arcade, crammed with kids in various stages of 'plugging in, switching on, and chilling out', Sipho recognises some of the best pals he has never met: a group of CyberFrenz from a VideoChat channel on the World Wide Web.

Somewhat awkwardly, they exchange greetings — like many kids his age, Sipho is more adept at CyberChatting than FaceTalking — before a soothing voice announces that the Socialisation Skills class is due to get underway in the Party Hall in exactly five minutes. Sipho dashes off with a mumbled 'later', but changes course when a giant video billboard catches his eye.

Hey, how about that class in Psyberchology, the science of studying and treating online addictions and obsessions? Or how about Two-Finger

Touch Typing, the almost lost art of communicating with a computer by keyboard rather than voice? No, decides Sipho. It's got to be Extra-Century Perception. Trekking through ancient history with a joystick and a pair of virtual reality goggles. Cool!

Sipho takes his seat in a room where the work stations have been arranged in concentric circles around a free-floating four-dimensional VideoBoard, which is hovering above a nest of infra-red servers and routers with satellite links to the Internet.

'Log in, please,' says a voice in the ether, and Sipho clenches his fist and holds it over a glowing red light on his metallic desktop. The sensor scans the microchip embedded inside his wrist, recognising and analysing the Individual Learner Profile on which his interests, achievements and aptitudes have been noted. The desktop slides open with a whoosh.

Sipho reaches into the hollow and pulls out what appears to be a slim hardcover exercise book used for double-entry book-keeping.

He opens it up. It's a computer. There's a touchpad with a voice-sensor at the bottom and a high-definition monitor at the top.

A professorial face beams a greeting: 'Hello, Sipho. Welcome to today's lesson.' The facilitator introduces himself. He's a TimeTrekking tutor at a Remote Learning Facility somewhere in Finland.

Funny, thinks Sipho. He doesn't sound Finnish. As the Babel Communications Interface translates the conversation, Sipho dons his VR goggles and narrows down his choice from the on-screen menu.

'Late twentieth century,' he says. 'People and Technology. Personal Computers. Education. South Africa.'

Sipho sits back. Wow! He can't believe his goggles. Did kids really go to school like that in the 1990s? Let's take a look for ourselves...

TRRRINNNGGG! One fine day in the late 1990s, the school bell echoes through the corridors of Parktown Boys' High in Johannesburg. It sounds the same as any other school bell, except for one thing: It's home time. But not every scholar hears it that way.

Some head for the playing fields to practise their rugby or cricket. Some stay behind to sharpen their skills at chess or debating. And some, quickening their step, taking the stairs two at a time, dash towards the most popular classroom — the computer lab.

Here, sitting at banks of multimedia Pentiums connected to the Internet, switched-on scholars can send and receive e-mail, explore the

World Wide Web, search CD-ROM encyclopaedias for useful information, and generally get their homework out of the way before they even get home.

What they're not allowed to do is have too much fun. This is, after all, a place of learning. The rules: no computer games, no unauthorised software installation, and definitely no straying from the straight and narrow paths of the information highway. Then again, there's no getting away from it. Computers are cool.

'I have no problems with *Battle Chess* or *SimCity*,' says Parktown computer master Denis Brandjes. 'But if I see a kid with a nude figure on his screen, he's going to have to do some pretty nifty talking to convince me it has anything to do with the Art curriculum. But it doesn't happen often. You don't need violent games or fantasies to make computing attractive to schoolchildren.'

At Parktown, one of the nation's most computer-wise schools, each student has his own e-mail address, a megabyte of storage space on a central file server, and after-hours access to the computer lab on a book-in-advance basis.

Students with a flair for numbers and a dream of becoming the next Bill Gates can opt to take Computer Science as an extra exam subject. They'll learn the history of mainframes and microprocessors, the bits and bytes of data storage, and the secrets of programming in PASCAL and COBOL.

Everyone else, technophobic teachers included, is encouraged to acquaint themselves with the basics of computer literacy, and the lab is also used for holiday activities and post-Matric courses. Parktown's investment in information technology is being put to good use. But it's only the beginning.

For Denis Brandjes, the real challenge is to shift the focus from the technology itself and turn computing into an all-round, integrated part of the curriculum.

'It's time we stopped seeing computers purely as scientific or mathematical instruments,' says Denis. 'We need to begin using them as creative, problem-solving devices across subjects and disciplines. Not just as accessories, but as real, practical tools for learning.'

Example? Denis scrawls an outline of an engineering project on a piece of paper. 'Let's say a student is given a project to design a suspension bridge.'

He could begin by researching famous bridges and bridge-builders on CD-ROM or the Internet. He might post a query to a newsgroup, or e-mail an international expert for advice. Once all the relevant information is at hand, he might turn to one program to calculate stresses and strains, and another to shape a 3-D model of his masterpiece. Finally, our student could use a word processor to write and format his report, and a multimedia presentation such as PowerPoint to make it come alive.

The way Denis sees it, computers are more than just machines. They're bridges between concept and reality, between information and understanding.

'Computers allow you to look at a problem from many different angles and solve it in many different ways. They encourage you to think logically and laterally and in several directions at once. They broaden your horizons and open up the world.'

Of course, there's a lot to be said for pen and paper too. For one thing, it's cheaper. By the year 2025, rest assured, today's bulky, exorbitant desktop machines will have evolved into sleek, ultra-powerful mini-PCs, no bigger or costlier than the textbooks they will rapidly replace. For now, housed in media centres or laboratories like objects of curiosity or scientific research, computers have a way of becoming their own worst enemies. They're hugely expensive to buy, maintain and run. They're finicky to operate, and highly susceptible to planned obsolescence. In the classroom, they tend to dominate the desktop and the conversation, drawing constant attention to themselves instead of getting on with the job.

Small wonder that some teachers view them more as a threat than a promise. Kate Poole, a Randburg high school teacher who runs a private after-school computer centre, defines the problem as a classic struggle between human and machine. 'Being a teacher puts you in a very powerful and commanding position,' she says. 'But when you're standing in front of a class of kids with computers, and their eyes are glued to the screen rather than the teacher or the blackboard, you're suddenly nowhere near as powerful as you thought you were. It can be a very disarming experience.'

Even at schools where computers are as commonplace as pencil cases, resistance from the Old Guard can be difficult to break down. At Sacred Heart College Primary School, a private school in Johannesburg, each classroom boasts at least five multimedia computers linked to the school's network and loaded with specialised educational software. Teachers are free to use the technology at their own discretion. If it's a Maths class, they might assign teams of pupils to run through a series of computer-based exercises, while the rest of the class will stick to pen, paper and textbook. If the subject is English, some pupils will pen their essays in longhand, while others will process their thoughts and words on a computer screen.

The idea, says computer teacher Lorraine Marnewick, is to 'demystify technology, not for the students, but for the teachers'. By setting computers free from laboratory conditions, the school hopes to incorporate them as naturally as possible into every aspect of the curriculum (with the possible exception of Physical Education).

'I would love the computer to lose its novelty in the classroom,' says Lorraine. 'I would love it to be seen as just another resource. Does it really matter what tool or method you use to solve a problem? I don't think so. What matters is understanding how and why you reached that particular solution.'

But for many teachers of the old school, the journey is just as important as the destination. What good does it do a child to get full marks for a Mathematics test if a computer takes care of all the calculations? How does a child benefit from a writing project if a computer takes care of all the spelling? Don't computers make you lazy? Don't they atrophy your own analytical skills? And what about your handwriting?

To anyone who went to school in the 1970s, these arguments will have a familiar ring for this was the era when the adding-machine married the microchip, and a cute little machine called the 'pocket calculator' was born.

Suddenly, instead of agonising for hours over the long-forgotten formula for dividing 975 by 42.6, all you had to do was hit a few buttons, and the answer would appear in a liquid-crystal flash (22,88732394366, of course — unless I hit the multiplication button by mistake).

The arrival of these battery-operated marvels, easy on the pocket in more ways than one, caused a quandary among educationists. Allowing them in the classroom, not to mention the exam room, would be the first step in creating a generation of innumerates, incapable of performing the simplest of calculations without electronic assistance.

Nonsense, ran the counter-argument. The machines were simply the latest in a long line of labour-saving devices, and were far more likely to awaken interest in Mathematics by eliminating much of the drudgery. As it turned out, both schools of thought were right. Many of us can't even add up a restaurant bill without calling for a calculator, and yet mathematical masterminds still manage to build suspension bridges and launch telescopes into space.

Likewise, today's computer children are probably already losing the ability to write neatly and legibly in the classic cursive style. If this trend continues, we may be left with a generation of children who are fit for nothing but careers in medicine or journalism. But it's too late to argue. The revolution is upon us, and it even has a name: TBLCE.

So what exactly is Technology-Based Learning-Centred Education? To begin with, it's a cautious acknowledgement that technology in the classroom doesn't begin or end with computers. Technology could be a TV set, a video recorder and a pile of educational tapes. It could be an overhead projector with sheafs of transparencies. It could even be a pocket calculator.

The idea is to use technology as an integrated aid to teaching — not just a means to an end, but as an object of study in itself. Curriculum 2005, the government's much-vaunted framework for 'Lifelong Learning', identifies technology as one of eight key learning areas for primary and secondary education. Among the goals: the effective use of technological products and systems; the demystification of technology; the recognition and respect of diverse technological solutions; the ability to evaluate products and processes from functional, economic, ethical, social and aesthetic points of view; and the delivery of quality education and access through integration of theory and practice in a changing modern world.

Phew! Somewhere in there, there must be room for a computer connected to the Internet. But with all that technology, will there still be room for teachers? Don't be crazy. Someone's still going to have to open the classroom door in the morning. The word 'facilitator' may not have quite as noble a ring as 'teacher', but it's already become an accepted part of the vocabulary of 21st-century education.

In a technology-based environment where the student might have access to a wide range of resources inside and outside the classroom, the teacher will no longer be the sole source of knowledge and information. The role of the teacher will be to guide, discuss, advise and facilitate; in many ways, the role of the teacher will be to learn.

That's why teachers like Denis Brandjes talk with passion about the new priority in the school curriculum: 'We've got to teach the teachers. So many of them are fearful of the new technology. They don't know how to use it, they don't know why they should use it, and they really don't want to know. But unless they at least begin exploring the possibilities, computers in schools are going to be nothing more than white elephants.'

Because schools are not obliged to make use of computers for any subject other than Computer Science, there are no official guidelines for their use. But the Parow Teachers' Centre in Cape Town, where tomorrow's teachers — sorry, facilitators — are taught, has compiled a handy checklist to guide school policy makers and other interested parties.

Next time you're asked to buy a cake or raffle ticket to help fund an extension to your school's computer centre, you might also want to put the following questions to the powers-that-be:

A computer centre checklist

1. Are pupils learning at the computer centre, or are they being taught? Real learning takes place when pupils are actively enquiring and experimenting while using computers. The teacher should merely be the facilitator.

2. Is there context to that learning? Are pupils, for example, learning to use a spreadsheet program because it is regarded by the teacher as a useful tool? That is not a good context. If they're learning to use the spreadsheet because they need to calculate data and draw graphs for a Geography project, then the context is good.

3. What degree of integration with the curriculum takes place in the school's computer literacy program?

4. What tools are available in the computer centre? Is there a CD-ROM? An Internet connection? A scanner? Is there a good quality inkjet or laser printer? If you do not have the resources, the computer cannot be a resource.

5. What social and personal skills are being developed in the computer centre? Computer skills will come with regular use of the computer. The real skills — educational, social, personal — must be developed during group interaction, and through authentic and challenging educational projects.

6. How much confidence and independence — in the context of computer use — do pupils develop through their experience in the computer centre? That's actually the broad aim of computer literacy: to enable pupils to go to high school, or to leave high school, with the confidence to be able to say, 'I am a computer confident person!'

Chapter 16

The wired classroom

Schools and the Internet

To get to Hoërskool Die Adelaar in Roodepoort, Gauteng, you head west on the Ontdekkers Highway from Johannesburg. You pass several shopping malls, factories, mine dumps and patches of veld set aside for Mediterranean-style cluster development.

Just before Krugersdorp, you turn left on Corlett. Then left into South, and left into Vermooten. You can't miss it. It's a typical two-storey fortress of learning, built the way schools have been built for generations. Rows of classrooms, with rows of desks, facing blackboards that squeak with inscriptions of knowledge.

There is the smell of chalk dust and the drone of declensions in the air. Here and there, a sign that high technology has crept its way into the curriculum: an overhead projector, with a silhouetted hand scrawling a mathematical formula in red or green felt-tip.

Now climb two flights of stairs, stroll down the concrete corridor, and step across the portal into a different world. Forget the blackboard. Ignore the dusty, dog-eared textbooks. Sit down and get ready to surf. You're in the Wired Classroom.

At the head of the class, six 586 computers, networked and connected by permanent digital line to the greatest classroom in the world — the Internet. Beyond the syllabus, beyond the walls, this is the gateway to a brave new world of information and understanding.

Take a tour of an art museum in Paris. Talk to a scientist in Antarctica. Dissect a virtual frog in California. Through the visual buzz and dynamically updated content of the World Wide Web, the lightning-fast communication of e-mail, and the anything-goes discussion forums of the Usenet newsgroups, the Internet can be a limitless source of inspiration and excitement for teachers and pupils alike.

Here, in between classes, sits Marina Myburgh. Teacher, trailblazer, evangelist for the power of the Internet in education. Officially, the subject Marina teaches at Die Adelaar is Computer Studies. Unofficially, it's Everything under the Sun. She puts her hand on the mouse and spins the cursor around the hyperlinks on a Web page. Click here, click there, click anywhere. The possibilities are endless.

'You know the really wonderful thing about the Internet? It makes you realise two things about the world we live in.' Click. 'How big it is, and how small it is.' Search for information or surf the Web at random, and you're awed by the vastness of the medium. Send e-mail to someone in another time zone, and the notion of distance disappears. Marina flips through the pages of a hefty textbook. 'It makes you feel that the world doesn't end here.'

She types the name of her school into a text box, and clicks on Search. Oceans away, a computer transmits the message to a piece of software, which begins scanning millions of documents on thousands of computers. The results come pouring in.

There are about 700 pupils at Die Adelaar, and only six computers connected to the Internet. And yet the school has become a model of what can be achieved by putting the technology to everyday use.

'It all began,' says Marina, 'with this little black box over here.' She points to the Cisco 2500 router, a sophisticated device for connecting computers to each other or the Internet. A router will set you back about R23 000. If somebody wants to give you one for nothing, you don't say no. Of course, this wasn't really for nothing; it was Die Adelaar's prize for finishing third in their category in CyberFair 96, an American-run Website competition open to schools around the world. Students are required to focus on interesting people, places or events in their communities, and then craft a site capable of conveying that interest to people in other countries. It's a working example of a principle at the heart of the Internet: Think locally; act globally.

Using a painfully slow 9600 modem and a borrowed computer, a group of Marina's pupils designed and submitted a site about the conservation of black eagles at the nearby Witwatersrand Botanical Gardens. More than anything else, the entry was an exercise in the application of a technology beyond Die Adelaar's means.

For years, the school had soldiered along with a pack of antiquated 386s. Mono screens, 8MB of RAM, no hard drives. Fine for running

Windows 3.1 and teaching the 'basic computer architecture' and programming skills required by the Computer Studies syllabus; useless for designing a Web page or connecting to the Internet. Then came the router. It was like giving a state-of-the-art video recorder to someone who has never had a television.

'When the man from Cisco came out to look at our setup,' says Marina, 'he was too polite to say anything, but I could see it in his eyes: "Ag, shame."'

There was only one thing to do: Buy a bunch of bigger, better, faster computers. So Marina went out and bought them.

Government schools have limited budgets, and other priorities. Die Adelaar needed a new school bus before it needed new computers. Marina's proposal: She would raise the finance and buy the computers. The school would lease them from her and foot the bill for the digital line to the Internet — about R2 000 a month. It took a lot of talking, but the investment has paid off.

CyberFair 97 drew more than 250 entries from primary and high school students in 37 countries. Winner of the Historical Landmarks category: Hoërskool Die Adelaar, Roodepoort. This time, Marina's pupils delved millions of years into the past for inspiration. They visited the Sterkfontein Caves, one of Africa's cradles of evolution. They took photographs, read books, interviewed experts. Then they put it on the Web for the world to see.

There is an essay on the genesis of man, with diversions on toolmaking and the discovery of fire. There is an animated graphic of the evolution of the species, and a revolving image of the skull of Mrs Ples. There are pictures scanned from magazines, and sound clips and a movie that can be downloaded as you read the text. One day, all school projects will look like this.

For now, what are the real spin-offs, aside from another visit from the friendly man from Cisco? Marina makes it clear. The Internet isn't just another Computer Studies subject. The Internet is a vehicle for teaching and learning. Everyone can come along for the ride. At Die Adelaar, the prize-winning Sterkfontein Caves project awakened enthusiasm among even the most difficult-to-convince sceptics. The Geography and History departments saw new ways of enlivening their subjects. The English department saw a powerful, vibrant medium for enhancing second-language skills. And the Computer Studies department, finally, saw a way of putting the theory of Data Communications into practice.

'There are benefits and applications across the curriculum,' says Marina. 'You learn to master the art of finding and organising information. You learn to integrate what you find on the Net with material from other sources. You develop your communication skills because you have to put your ideas across in a way that others will find interesting. You learn the value of teamwork because the Internet encourages the sharing of ideas and information. You improve your knowledge of computer hardware and software. You broaden your awareness and understanding of the world around you.'

More than anything else, as Marina was to discover, you broaden your awareness and understanding of the Internet itself. Aside from her Computer Studies classes, Marina teaches basic computer literacy to children across the school. They also have the option of using the computer centre after hours, with a nominal charge of R5 per half-hour for Internet access. To begin with, most kids had a vague idea of the nature of the Net. Some were 100 per cent certain.

'When word first got around that we had a permanent Internet line at the school, a lot of kids would come in here and say, "Okay, Miss, where are the games?" They were under the impression that the Internet is one big video game arcade. I had to show them that you can't play games until you find them, download them, and copy them to another computer.'

What? A computer teacher who allows her pupils to play games? Yes, because they're not just playing games. They're learning to use a computer. They're learning to click and drag with a mouse. Sooner or later, they'll want to move on to the real stuff.

'Kids definitely get bored with games after a while,' says Marina. 'That's why they can be a useful learning experience. If you just give someone a mouse and say, okay, use Netscape, they're going to be stuck.'

The rule is: no games on the Internet computers. If you're going to play around, play around on the 386s. The other rule is the usual one applied to kids who surf the untamed waters of the Web. The school uses software to block access to adults-only sites — 'If you ask for "sex", you get sent to Walt Disney Pictures' — but the real key is constant supervision.

'Every now and then you'll get a kid who manages to access a picture of someone like Cindy Crawford. And sometimes, she won't have too much on. Then again, it's all part of teaching a child. Everyone's curious about things like that. So you tell them, "Okay, fine, you've seen it, now let's move on."'

That doesn't just apply to supermodels. For schools that must come up with their own funding to equip computer centres, the battle to keep pace with technology can never be won. Marina Myburgh's 386s were once the epitome of speed and processing power. The programming languages she taught were once the industry standard. She knows that the same slide into planned obsolescence will one day turn her crop of superfast 586s into cumbersome antiques. But she's not complaining. She's on the frontline of the most exciting, most dynamic subject on the syllabus, empowered to explore an area of education that changes from day to day.

'I'm not a teacher,' she says. 'I'm a learner. I'm never afraid to say, "I don't know." I just say, "Let's find out."'

Chapter 17

The cyberteachers

Blazing a trail on the information highway

Browser the rhino took his name from the Net, but it was snail-mail that sent him to the other side of the planet. Amazingly, he arrived safely and settled down to a new life in Victoria, Australia. Meanwhile, Pokey the platypus found his way to Cape Town. In the shadow of Table Mountain, he was warmly welcomed and taken to heart by the Grade 2 pupils of Mickelfield Junior School. Cultural exchange? Sort of. In the real world, Browser and Pokey are nothing more than a pair of fluffy toys. On the Internet, they're 'Travel Buddies', keeping in touch and swapping tales through e-mail and the World Wide Web. In the process, the children who serve as their hosts get an insider's view of history, geography and everyday life — human and animal — in a far-away environment.

It's all part of the rich tapestry of education on the Internet, and for the cyberteachers who take pride in weaving the technology through the curriculum, it's the best thing to happen to teaching since ... well, since teaching began.

Margaret Dugmore teaches History and Computer Studies at Mickelfield. Her enthusiasm for the Internet, like the Internet itself, is boundless. She's taken her pupils on a cycling expedition through the jungles of Central America, following in the footsteps of the Ancient Maya. She's taken them game-spotting in Canada and Finland. She's led them on a quest to find tap-water in Iceland, and to feel the heat of the sun in Wodonga, Australia. They've written a horror story, paragraph by nail-biting paragraph, with students from a dozen different countries. All this without setting foot outside their computer laboratory in — as the Mickelfield home page puts it — 'picturesque Cape Town in sunny South Africa'.

Margaret Dugmore's pupils are lucky. They have instant, everyday access to a medium that has become the magic carpet of education. Their teacher, who proudly admits to being hooked on the Net, spends hours of her own time online, swapping ideas with other academics, signing her classes up for interactive projects, seeking new ways of reviving tired old subjects.

Teach a bunch of Sixth Graders history by the book and they'll battle to stay awake. Let them send e-mail to archaeologists on a dig or follow their day-by-day progress on the World Wide Web and the subject comes alive as they connect across the boundaries of time and space.

But let's get back to earth for a moment. In America, almost 70 per cent of schools have some kind of connection to the Internet, with the figure rising as government and private funding fuels the dream of the information superhighway. And in South Africa? By the time you read this, it's quite possible that the figure will have tripled — to reach almost three per cent.

Statistics compiled by Stephen Marquard, technical director of the Western Cape Schools' Network, show that the Western Cape is the most connected province, followed by Gauteng, the Eastern Cape and KwaZulu-Natal. The remaining provinces barely come into the picture.

Although a national schools' network has been mooted to generate funding and promote the use of the Internet as an educational tool, the initial target seems modest: 1 000 schools online by the end of the century. But there are reasons for that modesty. Money, for one. Aside from the hefty outlay for even a single computer, Internet access can cost a school anything between R100 and R2 000 a month. Systems have to be maintained and upgraded. Teachers have to be taught. Small wonder, as the draft national network proposal observes, that there has been a lack of demand for Internet access from schools with an 'inadequate awareness of the available benefits'. It's also safe to assume that many South African schools have other priorities when it comes to technology. Electricity, for instance.

But even for the tiny minority of connected schools, it's not always easy putting the benefits of the Internet into practise. Gill Summerley is the Cyberian — all right, the librarian — at St John's College in Houghton, Johannesburg. She believes the Internet can be a 'fantastic tool' for learning. But for teachers and children alike, she warns, the learning curve can be steep.

There are 12 computers in the school's library. Because of the heavy demand, pupils are allowed to use them for only half an hour at a time. When it comes to Internet access, Gills finds that time is often wasted. Pupils will surf the Net with no method or direction. Consequently, the only thing they'll get out of it is information overload. Gill makes it clear that she has nothing against surfing. But even surfers need to have some idea where the wave will take them.

'There are great benefits to serendipity,' she says. 'But you must have a starting-point, a point of reference. Even if it's just a hobby or passing interest. The kids who get the best use out of the Internet are those who have done some research beforehand, or at least have a clear idea of what they want to know. The rest just surf around in circles, until they wear themselves out. There's an enormous lack of appropriate skills. I think the time has come to re-look at the way we're using the Internet.'

It was with this in mind that Gill undertook the first comprehensive study of Internet access and use in South African schools. As part of an Honours degree research project into the potential benefits of the Internet as an educational resource, she sent an e-mail questionnaire to 222 schools that were 'officially' connected, mostly through regional or provincial networks. She received 35 responses.

Many of the schools, it turned out, were no longer connected. In the Free State, for instance, an education department subsidy had been lost, leaving not a single school online.

But even at schools that regularly use the Internet, the technology faces an uphill battle for acceptance. Gill's respondents reported that up to 75 per cent of teaching staff at their schools were 'computer shy', with many perceiving the Internet as a threat rather than a tool. Result: With the exception of a small group of trailblazers, South African schools are stuck on the hard shoulder of the information highway.

Part of the problem is the perception that the Internet is just the latest in a long line of loudly trumpeted panaceas for educational ills. The use of audiovisual media and the 'distance learning' concept proved to be major disappointments. Why should the Internet be any different?

For Gill, the answer lies in the Internet's combination of global connectivity within an information-rich environment. This isn't just a video recorder with a series of educational tapes. This isn't just a 30-minute question-and-answer session with a talking head in a television studio. This is the future. Gill outlines some of the ways the Internet can be used to enrich the learning experience:

Tele-access Browse through an online library, stroll through an online art gallery, learn a foreign language, explore the latest photographs from the Hubble telescope. Online resources, says Gill, allow pupils to 'construct their own knowledge' rather than them having to digest edited answers and information from a limited syllabus.

Tele-presence Without leaving their classrooms, pupils can experience events as they happen in locations across the globe. They can follow the path of a hurricane through constantly updated satellite images and the eyewitness accounts of their peers. They can collect and examine data from remote probes, whether the probes are across the road or on the moon. Adding video and sound allows students to journey on real expeditions and participate in real experiments. Gill points to the Live from Antarctica Project, which gave students daily access to the diaries and field journals of a group of polar scientists.

Tele-mentoring Thanks to the open-minded, open-ended nature of the Internet, many professionals are willing to share their knowledge with students through live chat forums and e-mail. Suddenly, it's not just one teacher standing in front of a classroom with a textbook and a stick of chalk.

Tele-sharing The Internet is not just a network of computers. It's a network of people. What begins as a simple exchange of greetings on a newsgroup or discussion forum can turn into a series of lively, almost limitless opportunities for sharing ideas, experiences, data and findings. As Gill explains, this type of 'one-to-one', 'one-to-many' or 'many-to-many' communication can shatter the boundaries of the traditional teacher–pupil relationship. On the Internet, it doesn't matter who or where in the world you are. What matters is what you have to say.

Tele-publishing Like no other medium in history, the Internet has wrested control of the global flow of information from the mega publishing conglomerates. Anyone with a computer and a modem can publish anything they want to on the Net, which is as much of a problem as it is an opportunity. Pupils can seize the opportunity by exposing their ideas to a global audience, in the process learning communication and computing skills that will give them an edge in the Age of Information.

The Internet is an evolving technology, and its use as an educational resource has only just begun to be explored. But already, Gill can see the long-term benefits. Through collaborative research and investigation, pupils learn to analyse, evaluate and interpret information in a new way. They learn not only how to ask the questions, but how to question the answers. They're no longer compelled to accept information at face value, since nothing on the Internet is sacred or set in stone. The Internet encourages pupils to look beyond their own classroom, community and country. Initially, they'll be sharply aware that they're communicating across oceans and national boundaries. But the Internet has a way of proving that those boundaries aren't real, and that people have more things in common than things that set them apart. Throught the Internet pupils are given the power to become their own teachers, while teachers are given the freedom to step beyond their traditionally didactic role. Learning all the while, they become guides, facilitators or 'co-investigators'. No wonder some teachers perceive the medium as a threat. For Gill, it's a promise — a pathway to making learning 'more relevant, meaningful and enjoyable' for everyone involved in the process.

The real challenge, of course, is to get everyone involved in the process. Let's take a look at one educator's proposal.

Chapter 18

The Internet without a net

Putting the Web to work in South African schools

'We don't need no education,' booms the chorus of voices on the campus of the hallowed Alma Mater. 'We don't need no thought control.'

A moment's pause for thought, and then the ground swell of youthful fury and contempt comes crashing through. 'Hey, teacher, leave us kids alone!'

Behind the microphone, the man with the spectacles chuckles quietly to himself. Edward P. Rybicki, Pink Floyd fan, freelance deejay and Associate Professor of Microbiology at the University of Cape Town, is taking a break from lectures and molecular analysis to spin a favourite platter for Campus Radio.

Ed agrees. We don't need no education. What we need is plenty of it. But not the old school, teaching by rote, learning by the dull thud of repetition. What we need is a way of teaching that opens the classroom, opens the mind, and lets the world come rushing in. What we need is the Internet.

As a researcher and educator, Ed wonders how he ever managed without it. The strands of the network, reaching across the globe, linking like minds in remote classrooms and laboratories, are embedded in his very DNA. It used to take him hours to submit a query on a DNA or protein sequence to the over-burdened mainframe computer on the UCT campus.

Now, using e-mail or the World Wide Web, he can retrieve the complex codes in seconds from the data bank of a supercomputer in the American state of Maryland.

Making quantum leaps from one server or work station to another, he can search for and retrieve abstracts of journal articles, and share knowledge and ideas with researchers all over the world. The result has been a radical shift in the way Ed works. But it doesn't end there.

As a teaching tool, the Net gives Ed and his students dynamic access to resources that were once far beyond reach. By clicking on the links in an interactive tutorial on the university's Web site, students can explore information databases in England and Australia, which in turn will link them to other sites with other links.

It's an endless cycle of learning and discovery, allowing students to work in their own time and at their own pace, with as much or as little deviation from the basic text as they choose. But even as Ed puts the technology to everyday use, he wonders how much use it can be in the real world.

In a society where many schools don't even have electricity, how can the benefits of the Net be brought into the classroom? Ed has given the matter a lot of lateral thought, and this is what he suggests. If schools don't have computers, take computers to schools. And if schools can't connect to the Internet, let them connect without the Net.

How? Firstly, by harnessing the power of HTML, the easy-to-learn programming language that allows text and graphics to be displayed and interlinked on the World Wide Web. You don't need an Internet connection to put HTML to work. What you need is a computer capable of running Windows, and a couple of pieces of freely available software: a Web browser and an HTML editor.

The editor allows you to reformat existing material and add scanned-in graphics to bring static text and line diagrams to life. By saving online text and images in HTML, you can easily store and link to them offline. Your Web browser will never know the difference. All the information would be stored on the computer's hard drive, but the multimedia effect could be as dynamic as anything on the Net. Maybe even better: You wouldn't have to wait for graphics to load, you wouldn't be subject to frustrating glitches on the network, and you could get away with using a computer as basic as a 386 notebook. Add a graphics projection tablet, an overhead projector and perhaps a CD-ROM drive and VCR, and you have what Ed calls 'the engine of a powerful and extremely portable means of teaching'.

So how would you drive the engine? The way Ed sees it, you'd simply pack your hardware into a vehicle and get the show on the road. You could do it on your own or you could outfit an old school bus or truck-

and-trailer as a mobile PC lab (a solution already put into gear by the University of the Western Cape). But the essence of the journey would lie in the software. You could show a class how deserts spread or continents move. You could show them cloud patterns shifting on a satellite map, or bacteria dividing and colonising, or Hollywood heroes putting drama into a dry scene from Shakespeare. You could visit several schools in one day, adapting and expanding the lessons as required. All it would take is a bit of editing on a batch of HTML files.

Okay, and a few other things. You'd need money, volunteers, equipment and the support of education authorities and the private sector. But Ed believes it can be done. The Net is too vast, and too alive with possibility, to be left in the hands of the techno-élite.

Getting the majority of South African schools online is a goal that will take years to fulfil. There are many other priorities. But by using basic, even outdated equipment, you can capture and condense the essence of the Internet for all to share. Ed would be the first to admit that he may be a pie-in-the-sky, ivory-tower academic who listens to too much Pink Floyd. But when he sees his own young kids using computers and surfing the Net, he begins to get an idea of what can and must be done.

'I am still sufficient of a child,' says Ed, 'to know what I would have preferred in my education, and what I would like for my children and their friends. Let us try and give it to them.'

Schools on the Web

Ever wondered what *Forti Nihil Difficilius* means? Or what it's like to go to school on a farm? Or how much it would cost to send your son to Hilton? Increasingly, you'll find the answers to these and other pressing questions on the World Wide Web as more and more South African schools take the online route to self-promotion.

Perhaps predictably, most school sites are studious and unexciting affairs, with pages devoted to History of School, Headmaster's Message, Rules of Discipline, School Anthem, Notable Achievements and — most yawnsome of all — Mission Statement.

Fortunately, there are several schools that dare to shatter the mould, producing sites that are colourful, spirited and — most important of all — interesting to outsiders. Herewith, a roundup of some of the coolest schools on the Net:

Afrikaanse Hoërskool Sasolburg
WWW address: http://cyberserv.co.za/users/~jako/affies.htm
Proudly Afrikaans — many Afrikaans schools choose to have English Web sites — the 'Affies' *tuisblad* features full text and photographs from the entertaining school newspaper, *Die Padda*.

Jeppe Boys' High School
WWW address: http://competition.global.co.za/jeppe/
Cool school, this. You can listen to a digitised rendition of a song by The Smashing Pumpkins as you browse more than a hundred years of history, including an account of the Great Fire that mercifully missed the computer centre.

Kloofwaters Intermediate School
WWW address:
http://www.gsn.org/web/models/cb/kloofh2o/index.htm
Fascinating, often touching insights into the daily life of a state-aided farm school in the North West Province, in the words and drawings of the pupils themselves.

South African College High School
WWW address: http://www.sacs.wcape.school.za/
A beautifully designed site, rich with graphics and information, including some interesting thoughts on why the birch rod should be brought back.

St David's Marist College
WWW address:
http://competition.global.co.za/StDavidsMaristCollege/
So well-designed and informative, one is almost tempted to overlook the misplaced apostrophes on the opening page.

St Stithians College
WWW address: http://competition.global.co.za/StStithians/
Most school sites, this site observes, are 'boring, boring, boring, boring, boring'. This one isn't. Cool features include a list of teachers' nicknames and a scholar's view of the curriculum: 'In Biology we cut open animals and stuff — if you like blood, take Biology!'

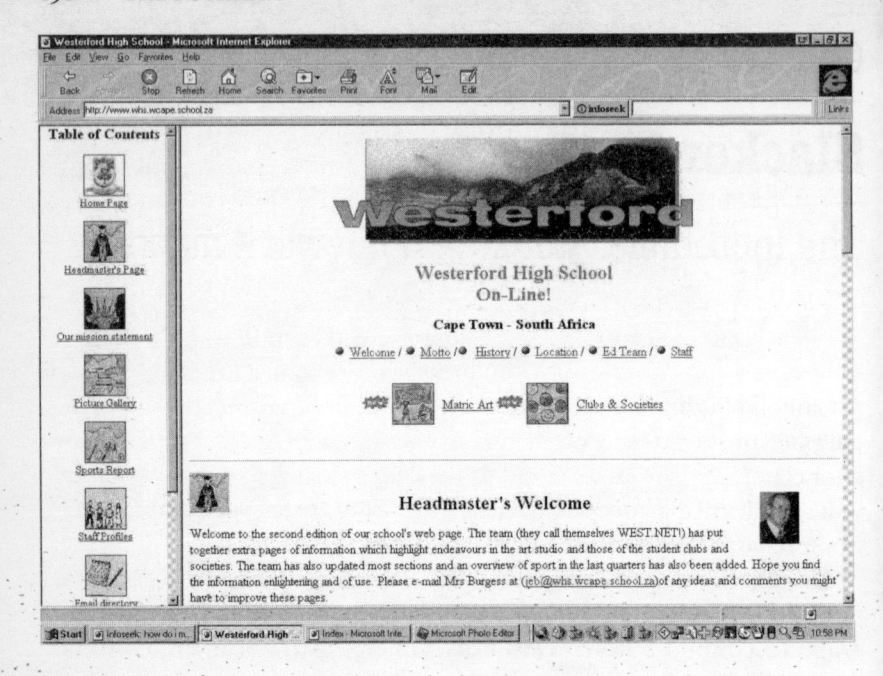

Westerford High School
WWW address: http://www.whs.wcape.school.za/
Cartoons, commentary, paintings and a portrait gallery of smiling teachers make this one of the most cheerful school sites on the Web.

The Wykeham Collegiate
WWW address: http://www.twc.pmb.school.za/
Wow! Great photographs, crisp copy, slick layout. On a par with the best corporate sites, this is a superb example of what a school can achieve if it has the money or clout to hire a professional Web design team.

Chapter 19

Slacker heaven

The incredible, amazing homework machine

A Gauteng high school teacher, shaking her head at the challenges facing her profession, recounts a conversation overheard in a corridor after class. Says one 15-year-old to the other: 'Just get your folks to buy you a multimedia computer, man. They only cost seven grand. You'll never have to do your homework again.'

Earlier, the student had handed in an assignment on environmental pollution. It was a masterpiece of visual presentation: laser-printed graphics, colour-coded spreadsheets, tables, charts, three-dimensional diagrams. Straight away, the teacher could see how much effort had gone into the project. After all, she, too, had a multimedia computer at home. She knew that the student had to:
1. switch on the computer
2. insert *Microsoft Encarta* in the CD-ROM drive
3. click on the Find button
4. type 'pollution' in the text box
5. go to the article on pollution
6. click on the Print button
7. lightly apply Pritt to the back of the pages, and paste them in the correct sequence on a piece of white poster paper.

So what else is new? In pre-PC days, panic-stricken scholars would gather *Brittanicas* and swarm around the public library's photostat machine, or persuade their loving parents to flip through magazines for photographs of mercury-poisoned fish. Cut and paste has always been the enterprising scholar's solution to the agonies of homework assignments.

And yet, something subtle has changed. In the Age of the Internet, the ancient schoolboy dream of a machine that will do your homework while you go out to play has come true at last. Even better: You can stay inside and play. Simply open up a window and double-click on *Doom*, while your trusty laser-printer churns out reams and reams of the boring stuff. (Computer experts call this 'multitasking'.)

But forget about CD-ROM encyclopaedias. Teachers aren't that dumb. Even the old-fashioned variety will begin to suspect something is amiss when the third assignment in a row turns out to be a carbon copy of an article with the author's name and copyright notice unapologetically intact.

But the Internet is different. Properly used, it can be a 'homework helper' of the highest quality, rewarding the disciplined, finely focused researcher with masses of pertinent data, opinion and possibilities for further exploration.

But who needs a homework helper when you can just as easily help yourself to somebody else's homework? I remembered reading somewhere — most likely on the Internet — that schoolkids were using the Net to redistribute term papers, projects, essays and homework assignments for the benefit of their peers around the globe. It sounded like a noble idea, true to the Internet's most egalitarian principle — the sharing of information in pursuit of greater understanding among the peoples of the world. It also sounded too good to be true. Could anyone be that devoid of scruples or personal pride as to copy somebody else's homework and present it as their own? I decided to put this to the test.

In the interests of research, I put myself in the place of a typical teenager who has until tomorrow morning to compile and present an in-depth assignment on a subject about which he knows nothing, and cares even less.

Let's see: 'The Impact of Chlorofluorocarbons on the Ecology of the Ozone Layer'. Where do I begin? I could try the library. But the library's closed. (Actually, I'm not even sure where the library is.) Fortunately, my folks, eager to provide me with every possible educational advantage, have been kind enough to buy me a multimedia computer with an Internet connection.

I decide against *Microsoft Encarta*. I'm going to be original for a change. I go online. Start my Web browser. Surf around a little. Read my e-mail. Chat to a buddy. Chat to a total stranger. Download a demonstration edition of *Need for Speed II*. Finally, at about 11.15 pm, I begin typing 'chlorofluourocarbons' into an Internet search engine. It's a long word. I spell it wrong. Midway through my second attempt, I am struck by a sudden flash of lateral thought. What if…? I begin typing a selection of relevant words into the search engine: homework, homework assignment, homework help, school project, research papers.

Hmmm … I don't seem to be making myself clear. I put my query in plain English: 'I'm looking for research papers to help me with my homework.' Bingo. In two clicks, I find myself at Research Papers Online: 'Instant gratification! The ultimate online resource for all your term paper needs. Our papers are new, written by professional writers, and have NEVER BEEN CIRCULATED BEFORE!'

Here are papers, thousands of words long, on everything from 'Affirmative Action' to 'What the French Peasants Wanted and Got out of the French Revolution' to 'Different Silvicultural Management Options to Save the Red Cockaded Woodpecker'. A peek at the contents reveals an impressive degree of depth, detail and understanding, combined with copious use of the personal pronoun. Even the grammar and spelling seem correct.

It is slacker heaven. Maximum marks for minimum effort. No way will teacher ever know that the 'I' so often referred to is, in fact, an anonymous researcher on the other side of the planet. And yet, there is something deeply immoral about the very concept of Research Papers Online. These guys want to charge you to rip off their work! For Affirmative Action alone, they're asking $54,95. Whatever happened to freedom of information?

I try another link. Ah. More like it: 'School Sucks'. Motto: 'Download Your Workload'. Working on the premise that the education system itself is antiquated, corrupt, misguided and incapable of inspiring or sustaining original thought, School Sucks offers absolutely free papers and essays on subjects common to curricula across the globe.

Trouble is, you get what you pay for. Shallow, semi-literate, factually challenged, the papers available on School Sucks appear to have been posted by the kind of students who would need to use a service like School Sucks in the first place. Herewith, an excerpt from an essay on 'Apartheid in Modern South Africa':

The discovery of gold and diamonds in South Africa during the 19th Century, ultimately lead to racially segregated compounds for mine workers becoming the fore fathers of apartheid. Today apartheid approaches its final years as political supporters of anti-apartheid such as President Nelson Mandela continually fights for a multiracial South Africa.

The political support of the antiapartheid movement was perhaps seen greatest in 1991. Written in Time Magazine by Greenwald, Former President F. W. de Klerk in February 1991 opened Parliament with a pledge to legalize the militantly antiapartheid African National Congress.

The political end of South Africa looks in support of antiapartheid whereas the few who don't, condone violent actions taken place against the antiapartheid supporters.

Certainly, any student presenting an essay of that standard would be unlikely to be accused of plagiarism. But there are exceptions to the rule. The Philosophy Department of School Sucks offers, without the slightest trace of irony, a well-crafted and cogently argued essay on 'Risk-Taking and Self-Command' — ethical dilemmas in contemporary society.

So where's the risk? It's so easy to find what you're looking for on the Net, so easy to copy it and cover your tracks, that even the brightest student may be tempted to abdicate self-command and let the computer do all the thinking. In the Analogue Age, if you copied an article from an encyclopaedia, the very least you had to do was read what you were copying.

But now, you don't have to understand or absorb. You only have to process. What's the solution? Simple. *Think.* That goes for teachers as well. Denis Brandjes, Computer Master at Parktown Boys' High, recalls a teacher who came running to him in alarm, bearing sheafs of papers as evidence. She had set her class a project, only to discover that several of the pupils had simply copied the same information from the same Web site at the computer centre after school.

Denis wasn't surprised. 'I told her she hadn't worded the project properly. It was too generic, too easy to answer by cutting and pasting from the Net. She couldn't fail the kids — after all, they had come up with the correct information. But she'd learned a lesson.'

Here it is. Don't make information-gathering the object of the exercise. Make it the starting-point. Once students have mastered the art of finding information, let them move on to the real challenge: finding out what it means. Let them analyse, interpret, draw conclusions, ask questions, and dig beneath the surface of the facts to get at the truth. A scholar with any sense of self-respect would never dream of carbon-copying someone else's work and presenting it as their own. But just in case, it may be a good idea for parents and teachers to acquaint themselves with these founts of second-hand wisdom. And don't worry about your kids. They've probably been there already.

Evil House of Cheat
WWW address: http://www.cheathouse.com/
No such thing as a free lunch here. You have to submit a paper of your own before you can access the 'master database'. Wonder if they have anything on Faust?

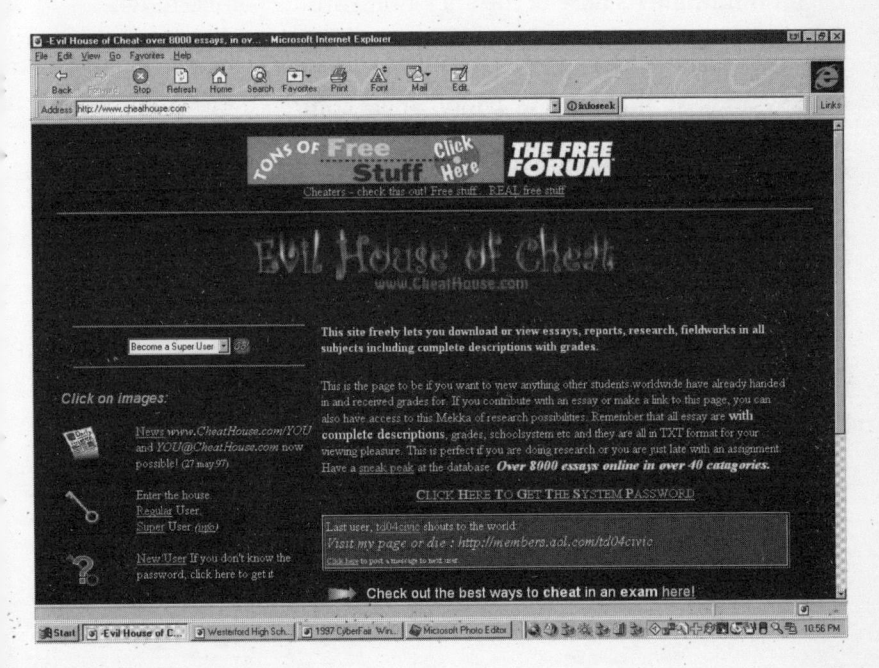

The Homework Homepage
WWW address: http://indigo.ie/~darkstar/
The disclaimer says it's simply a showcase for papers, projects and essays from around the globe. The object of the exercise is to 'pick out

the interesting pieces' and use them as inspiration for your own work. Yeah, right.

Research Papers Online
WWW address: http://www.ezwrite.com/ezw-bin/webmate/Store_1/form/ezwrite/column_store_template
Unashamed masters of the art of unattributed research. They'll even custom-write a thesis or dissertation for you. Quick! Hide that credit card!

Schools Sucks
WWW address: http://www.schoolsucks.com
'Disgusting', 'Disturbing', 'Despicable'. Just some of the rave reviews that have poured in from the academic community since this site began thumbing its nose at the ancient institution of learning.

The Source
WWW address: http://www.schoolpapers.com/
This is where I found my paper on CFCs. A well-organised site that tries hard to be respectable.

Term Papers for Free
WWW address: http://www.openix.com/~bytor/
'I personally take no responsibility if you fail, get suspended or expelled for using this,' disclaims the compiler of this raw list of text files on an FTP site.

Chapter 20

Teach your children

Computers and the homeschool revolution

It's 8 am in the suburb of Halfway Gardens in Midrand. The rush is almost over. The diesel-belching busses have off-loaded their uniformed cargo; the Taxi Moms have made their last-minute dashes; the stragglers, still catching up yesterday's homework, have sprinted to beat the bell and the threat of detention. Soon, the wrought-iron gates will swing shut and another day of organised education will begin.

But here in the Lancaster household, Cara (10) and her sister Megan (8) are taking it easy. It's been months since they waved goodbye to the world of teachers and timetables and chalk squeaking on blackboards. For them, school means something more than a building down the road. School means home.

Another hour will pass before the girls leave the breakfast nook and wander into the study, where the morning sun is at its warmest. Their mother, Karen, will join them. They will sit around a table laden with books and magazines and pens and pencils and crayons.

In the middle, humming quietly to itself, the Lancasters' gateway to a world of learning: a Pentium computer with a dial-up connection to the Internet. Karen consults her curriculum.

As usual, while minds are fresh and eager, the day begins with practical tuition in English and Maths. Then, the all-encompassing subject that will take them through to close of class at 12.30 pm. Yesterday it was Spanish. The day before, Science. What will it be today? 'Scotland,' decides Karen. She types the word into an Internet search engine, and the girls point excitedly at the screen as responses come flooding in.

Mom peruses the list, clicking on links to interactive maps, myths, legends, castles, bagpipes and the Highland fling. Across oceans and time zones, the history and culture of a faraway land come to life. With a point and a click, the basics of geography are brought home.

Mom reaches for a CD-ROM encyclopaedia, and the lives of great Scots — poets, artists, engineers — become the starting-point for lessons that embrace the spectrum of human knowledge. Spontaneity and serendipity lead the way.

A picture of Loch Lomond may provide the necessary spur for a heavily accented sing-a-long. A clan tartan may inspire a hands-on exercise in interior design. A portrait of the Loch Ness Monster may lead to a close encounter with a brontosaurus. Cara and Megan don't go to school any more. But they haven't stopped learning. And nor have their parents.

Karen and Bruce Lancaster, who help run a church in Midrand, are discovering for themselves the benefits, challenges and rewards of an educational revolution that is sweeping the globe — homeschooling. It's nothing new. Think of the bearded patriarch, at home in the wilderness, gathering his brood around the hearth to impart the fundamentals of reading, writing and arithmetic. Put a computer in place of the hearth, add a connection to the Internet, and you begin to get the picture. Homeschooling has gone high-tech. Computers have liberated information from libraries and schoolrooms. The Internet has bridged the distance between nations and cultures. Learning, the lifelong journey, has breached the barriers of an age-old institution.

The medium has changed, but the message remains the same: You don't have to send your kids to school to give them an education. At first, this sounds like a radical notion. Why school your kids at home when schools are built and teachers are trained to do the job for you? Why go against the grain of a system that has been tried and tested over hundreds of years? For many parents the answer is simple: Education is too important, and too personal, to leave to public educators.

Parents are natural teachers. Children are natural learners. For the first five or six years, you teach your children at home. Then you hand that responsibility over to a state or private school. Homeschooling allows parents to reclaim that responsibility by educating their children according to their own lifestyles, philosophies, and religious or political agendas.

But is homeschooling legal in South Africa? Yes. It's right there in Section 50 of the South African Schools Bill of 1996: 'A parent may apply to the Head of Department for the registration of a learner to receive education at the learner's home.'

The bill is vague on specifics, but it does lay down certain conditions. The Head of Department must be satisfied that registration is in the 'interests of the learner'. The education likely to be received at home must meet the minimum requirements of the public school curriculum, and must be of a standard 'not inferior to the standard of education provided at public schools'.

The Lancasters saw no problems in meeting those criteria. But to be on the safe side, they applied for registration through a private school, which monitors the children's progress and takes care of the legalities.

The system, says Karen, seems to be working. Her daughters are thriving. The hard part hasn't been homeschooling but un-schooling — getting years of public education out of their system.

'They were struggling at school,' says Karen, 'and we were always being sent off to test them at this occupational therapist and that educational specialist. One would insist that my daughter had eye coordination problems, another would say the opposite. I got tired of receiving no concrete answers, and nothing explained to me in layman's terms. Finally, I saw my younger daughter, who I know to be intelligent, withdrawing at school and only performing to the bare minimum.'

Karen recognised herself in those symptoms. 'My own school career was just so. Scrape through by doing the least work possible. I hated the system whereby everyone was expected to come up with the same answers, cookie-cutter style. I acknowledge that the government's new school curriculum may change things, but how long before it's properly implemented? Our kids couldn't afford to wait.'

After speaking to other homeschooling parents and researching the subject thoroughly on the Internet, Karen decided to base her children's education on an American curriculum. It takes care of the three Rs, and allows ample room for adaptation to local needs and conditions.

Out goes Social Studies, which Karen describes as 'all about Stars and Stripes and patriotism'; in comes Countries of the World. As part of their church work, the Lancasters travel extensively throughout Africa. Previously, Cara and Megan had to stay behind. Now, coming along is part of the curriculum.

'When we're planning a trip, we incorporate it into the schooling for weeks beforehand. We'll learn about the people, the culture, the land and the language. The girls will learn by seeing and doing, and they'll still be able to keep up with their other subjects while we're on the road.

It's fun, it's interesting, it's practical — and it helps keep us together as a family.'

Nothing wrong with that, of course. But for the growing band of work-from-home parents, who are most likely to look at homeschooling as an educational option, isn't there just a slight possibility that all that family togetherness can be too much of a good thing? The traditional school system may have its flaws, but at least it keeps parents and kids out of each other's hair for a few hours a day. Karen weighs up the pros and cons.

'I would say that homeschooling has had a very positive effect on our relationships within the family. The downside is that we can occasionally irritate each other. The girls sometimes bicker in the middle of work, or they don't want to do their lessons, which can be really annoying. And there are times when I desperately need a break. But on the whole, it has made me appreciate my children, and enjoy their company even more.'

Over to America, home of homeschooling. (They even invented the word.) As many as a million families homeschool their children there, some for religious or political reasons, some because of increasing violence and falling standards at public schools.

But more often, it's simply a case of the schoolchild not fitting into the school system. Willy Chaplin, a computer programmer and consultant based in California, decided to homeschool his teenage son, Roger, when it became clear that school was 'rapidly extinguishing his sense of wonderment in learning'.

Roger (17) puts it more bluntly: 'I think I'd be dead if I hadn't managed to get out of the public school rat race. I don't mean to be bitter, but public schools are run like prisons, or like some mad playground in an asylum.'

So Roger came home from high school, rediscovering his joy of learning through books, computers and the maddest playground of them all: the Internet. As part of a homeschool project, Roger once set out to design a Web site that would reflect his passionate interest in movies.

The result was Teen Movie Critic, a hugely successful compendium of reviews that put Roger on the map, and paved the way for a possible career in the movie industry. But if he's really learned anything from being schooled at home, it's how to learn on his own.

With both parents working from home, Roger was given the option of setting his own timetable rather than face the public school prospect of constant supervision. He chose: Maths on Mondays and Tuesdays; Science on Wednesdays; History on Thursdays; English and Literature on Fridays. In-between: kick boxing and swimming and surfing the Net.

'Basically, I make my own hours,' says Roger. 'I make sure I study for at least three hours a day, and I set myself assignments, which I'll show to my parents as proof of what I've learned. But that's all I *have* to do. The point is, I'm actually learning something, instead of just sitting in a classroom pretending to learn.'

Growing up with a computer-crazy father, Roger had access to computers from the day he was born. They've sparked his curiosity, accelerated his learning, and given him the freedom to pursue his own interests and ambitions.

'Let your kids use computers to the max,' advises Willy Chaplin. 'Let them roam as freely as they can. They can only be preparing for a future in which everyone will be computer literate.'

Willy agrees that homeschooling has brought the family closer together, but he also sees a downside: 'Roger's social development has been retarded with people his own age.'

Socialisation. It's a hot topic among homeschoolers, who defy conventional wisdom by educating children in isolation from their peers. For generations, schools have grouped pupils according to their age. They learn together, play together, develop together the social skills that will prepare them for adulthood. It makes sense. Or does it?

Marvin Minsky, former director of the Massachusetts Institute of Technology, and a renowned researcher on artificial intelligence, believes otherwise. 'Much of what we call education is really socialisation,' he argues. 'Is it really a good idea to send your six-year-old into a room full of six-year-olds, and then, the next year, to put your seven-year-old into a room full of seven-year-olds? Our present culture may be largely shaped by this strange idea of isolating children's thought from adult thought.

'Perhaps the way our culture educates its children better explains why most come out as dumb as they do, than it explains how some come out as smart as they do.'

Minsky points out a recurring theme in studies of the origin and nature of child genius. 'Most of them had an enormous amount of attention paid to them by one or both parents ... and generally they were relatively isolated from other children.'

This doesn't mean that a homeschooled child will automatically turn into a genius. Nor does it mean that a homeschooled child will automatically turn into a social misfit. What it does mean is that you have to strike a balance.

Says Miles O'Neal, a Texas-based dentist and homeschooling advocate: 'The point of school is primarily to learn. While kids do socialise there, if that's the main emphasis, the school is broken and I wouldn't want my kids there. If it's a minor part, then what's the big deal? My kids play with other kids after school and on weekends. They go on group outings and field trips. They're just like any other kids.'

Back in Midrand, Karen Lancaster makes sure her kids aren't housebound by arranging regular outings and get-togethers with other homeschooling families.

'I make it part of their learning. The girls will give speeches and presentations on what they're studying at home, or we'll go as a group to a game reserve and use it as the basis for lessons on a variety of subjects.'

Once you've accepted the notion that your kids don't have to go to school to get an education, you can take them anywhere. In the process, you too can get an education. Karen joins her girls for art classes once a week, and she's signed the family up for a course on using the Internet.

With this in mind, the Lancasters have also decided to invest in a second computer. 'We're saving a fortune on school fees,' says Karen. 'We may as well put it to good use.'

Right now, the Lancasters are among only a handful of South African parents who have opted to homeschool their children. But as technology makes it easier to bring information and knowledge into the home, and as parents grow more and more disenchanted with the public education system, schooling from home could one day be as common as working from home.

Clearly, it's not an option for everybody. Aside from the practical considerations, homeschooling requires vast reserves of patience, imagination, commitment, motivation, curiosity, fearlessness and trust between parents and children. But the rewards of learning in freedom can last a lifetime.

Grace Sylvan of San Jose, software developer and mother-of-two, has this advice for aspirant homeschoolers: 'Make it fun, for you and the kids. Don't simply try to reproduce school at home. Teach your children that learning is fun, and an everyday part of life. Then they'll be able to learn whatever they need to when they need it.'

Adds Karen: 'When I tell other parents that I school my children at home, the standard reaction is, "Wow, that's fantastic, but I could never do it." The point is, they could. It all comes down to instilling in your children a love of discovery and learning. If you can get that right, your children are ready to take on the world.'

Homeschooling sites on the Internet
Homeschooling Zone
WWW address: http://www.caro.net/~joespa/E_homskl.htm#toc2
A bright and breezy site, full of the joys of learning, with items of interest and value to parents, teachers and kids alike.

Jon's Homeschool Resource Page
WWW address: http://www.midnightbeach.com/hs/
As Jon himself admits, this is *the* homeschooling home page on the World Wide Web. It's well organised, informative and always up to date. Make it your first stop on the homeschooling highway.

School Is Dead, Learn in Freedom! Page
WWW address: http://www.concentric.net/~kmbunday/
Homeschooling propaganda at its most impassioned, with an exhaustive list of annotated links, facts and figures, and plenty of provocative opinion.

For further advice, insights and occasional invective on homeschooling and related issues[†], subscribe to the following Usenet newsgroup: misc.education.home-school.misc. The broad-based parenting newsgroup misc.kids can also be a mine of useful information on the subject, but is more often a battlefield between pro- and anti-homeschooling activists.

[†] For further information on the legalities of homeschooling in South Africa, contact the Department of Education in Pretoria on (012) 312-5911.

Chapter 21

Computer tutors of the future

The private tuition option

'I know! I know! I know!'

Fingers clicking like castanets, three eager eight-year-olds compete for the right to answer a high-tech riddle, guaranteed to boggle the brain of any watching grown-up. Why is that little arrow on the computer screen called a 'cursor', rather than, say, a 'little arrow'? Seems obvious enough. The more you try and jiggle it around the screen, the more it makes you curse.

But no: 'It's called a cursor because it's not always an arrow,' offers the moppet with the Shirley Temple curls.

'Yes, sometimes it's a dinosaur or a green thing with bubbles,' adds the spiky-haired co-user of her powerful Pentium PC.

That out of the way, hands hovering over keyboards, fingers itching to click cursors into action, the class of the future gets down to some serious personal computing. Today's assignment: Design and produce a Happy Easter card for a parent or best friend. It's 4 pm. School's out.

But here in the backroom of a suburban shopping centre, education, sneakily disguised as fun, is moulding young minds for the challenges of tomorrow. That, at least, is the premise behind Futurekids, one of many private computer tutoring operations springing up across South Africa.

As schools battle to keep pace with the computer revolution, these extracurricular centres seek to acquaint children with the fundamentals of computing, instil a sense of wonder and enthusiasm for information technology, and equip young minds with the knowledge and skills to get ahead in a changing global village. The future's so bright, you can see your face in it.

A shimmering sliver of glass and resin catches the light. 'Why,' asks teacher, 'do we call this a CD-ROM?'

A studious six-year-old hazards a guess: 'Because it's a CD but you don't put it in your hi-fi.'

Close enough. Now how about the ROM part? Stands for ... come on, you learned this last week...

'Disk Operating System!' volunteers the boy with glasses. Whoops. Right lesson, wrong acronym.

It's Compact Disc Read Only Memory, of course, as the disc slides into the drive and a double mouse-click fires up the software that will turn Easter wishes into inkjet-printed tokens of a child's dearest devotion. Parents and best friends will be wide-eyed with gratitude, and a child's own work will be affixed with pride to a billboard or refrigerator door.

And yet, for all the gusto and dexterity with which the project is tackled, it's hard to escape the notion that nothing beats scissors, paper, paste and paint when it comes to personal expression. Forget it. That's an old-world, old-school approach to the equation, which has nothing to do with How to Design a Happy Easter Card, and everything to do with How to Use a Computer.

Step number one: Switch it on. From there, according to the Futurekids syllabus, all it takes is another 749 separate skills to equip a 3- to 15-year-old with the power to master tomorrow's technology. Taught by rote, and using hand–eye co-ordination drills and homework assignments, computer literacy would be almost as much fun as trigonometry.

But teach it in the context of a bright, snappy, software program, and the learning is sweetened in the process of discovery and creation. Let's get back to that Happy Easter card.

By the time the inkjet printer zaps out the finished product, the junior artists will be capable of teaching their parents an impressive range of basic computer skills: how to insert a CD-ROM in the drive; how to select and open a program under Windows 95; how to format text and pictures; how to click, drag and scroll with a mouse.

Perhaps even more importantly, they will have learned something vital about the art of learning. Two heads are better than one. Teamed into twos, the children share a computer, printer, mouse and the first stirrings of expert knowledge, often without the teacher's intervention. It's called 'collaborative learning', and it's the axis on which the Futurekids curriculum turns. But it's not the only way.

At some centres, such as K-Net, sharing is out and individual learning is in. Which is best for your child? Since private computer classes fall outside the ambit of education departments, philosophies, facilities and teaching methods vary widely. If parents can afford the fees (anything from R50 to R250 a month), there's a lot to be gained from these once-a-week excursions into the fun side of computing.

But before you sign on the line, take time to examine a couple of things, beginning with your motives. Are you doing it because you want your child to be exposed to learning opportunities limited or denied in the school classroom?

Is it because you're impressed by claims of 'boosted self-esteem', 'increased social interaction skills' and 'enhanced academic ability'? Or is it just because the kid across the road wears a Futurekids T-shirt?

Private computer classes may be the trendiest extracurricular activity since rollerblading, but be wary of the subtle way they play on peer pressure and parental guilt. It's true that a self-confident, socially interactive, academically bright child may also be a computer-literate child, but the reverse doesn't necessarily apply. So don't expect miracles. Don't expect anything: Go along and find out for yourself.

Computer tutor checklist

The environment Whether it's in a shopping centre, office-block or private home, does the computer learning centre look safe and secure? Is the classroom bright, airy and adequately lit?

The furnishings Are they 'kid-friendly'? Are the tables low enough? Is there room to move, particularly if kids are sharing computers? Are the chairs comfortable, and can they be adjusted to suit even the most low-down toddlers? If not, are baby-chairs available? Is there a separate, supervised play area for younger children who may want a break from computing?

The computers Are there enough to go around? (Two children per computer is collaborative learning. Three or more is war.) Are the computers powerful enough to cope with today's demanding multimedia applications? (On less than a fast 486, they're not teaching computing, they're teaching history.) Are the computers networked, making it easier to share information and peripherals such as printers?

The peripherals Do they have at least one high-quality, colour inkjet printer? Is there a scanner? Are there modems for Internet access?

The philosophy What are the centre's aims and goals? How does it hope to achieve them? What claims does it make about the benefits of computer education for kids?

The lessons How long are they? (An hour is the norm, but half an hour is usually enough for toddlers.) Are the lessons structured in modules, or are they self-contained? Are they based on a recognised educational curriculum? Are they geared towards helping kids with their schoolwork? Are technical concepts communicated in an easy-to-understand way? Most importantly, are the lessons fun? And for more computer-savvy kids, are there opportunities for further study in fields such as programming and Web site designing?

The teachers What are their qualifications? What is their experience with computers? Aside from being *au fait* with the intricacies of information technology, how sensitive are they to the needs of children?

The software Is there a good range of up-to-date learning and creativity programs for kids of all ages? Is there a mix of children's programs and 'real world' applications, such as word processors and spreadsheets? Is the software used by the centre easily available on the retail shelves? (Some centres double as dealers, and will gladly sell you software and hardware for home use. But shop around to make sure you're getting a good deal.)

The free demonstration And the most important question of all: Do you get a free demonstration lesson for your child, with no obligations or strings attached? Don't be shy to ask. With that in mind, let's take a closer look at some of the options.

Futurekids: mastering the power

The revolution has begun. In chubby pink letters on a pitch-black background, the battlecry has been pinned to the wall: 'Futurekids Will Rule the World!'

Here's one right now.

He strolls into the office of the commander-in-chief, Philips screwdriver in hand. He whispers something about an internal modem. He finds what he's looking for and goes off to do his duty, takkies squeaking on the floor. His name is Jared Plumstead, he's 14 years old, and his dad's in charge around here.

Mike Plumstead is national director of Futurekids SA, the South African arm of an organisation that rules the world, at least when it comes to private computer tuition for children between 3 and 15. Launched in Los Angeles in 1983, by expatriate South African software developer Peter Markovitz, Futurekids has become a model for fun through learning, and learning through fun.

What's the secret? Slick branding, meticulous attention to detail, and an almost evangelical faith in the future of children and computers. The personal computer was still in its infancy when Peter Markovitz saw a gap in the market for child-centred education, and the advent of multimedia and the Internet have turned his vision into the commonplace.

Futurekids aims to give kids a similar head start, equipping them to 'master the world by mastering the power of computers'. Explains Plumstead: 'We take the mystery and abstraction out of a technological skill, making it understandable in a three-dimensional environment. We don't just teach kids how to use computer applications. We teach them how to use computer technology, holistically and in the real world.'

It sounds like serious business. It is. But the bottom line, the real secret, is fun. Gaming software is forbidden at Futurekids, but the American-designed syllabus makes up for it by turning everything into a game.

On a mission to save the world, let alone rule it, Futurekids are sent on assignment to remote jungles, crime-ridden cities, hospital emergency rooms, financial capitals and the tangled Web of cyberspace. Gathering data, information and insights along the way, they learn a wide range of computing skills, from word processing to graphics to database management.

These themed adventures give Futurekids the air of a virtual Disneyland. But the fun has a more serious spin-off: By learning to master computer technology, kids develop confidence and self-esteem, and the power to succeed academically.

Whatever the truth of that claim, Futurekids resists putting it to the test in its own environment. 'We're not a school,' stresses Plumstead. 'We don't give homework or encourage kids to compete against each other.'

Instead, if a class pulls off an assignment with particular enthusiasm and aplomb, equal reward will be dispensed in the form of 'Megabyte' tokens, which can be pasted into Futurekids passports and exchanged for Futurekids T-shirts, bags, caps and other trendy items, turning each kid into a walking advertisement for the company that will one day take over the world.

Tel: 0800-11-32-22 (toll-free)
E-mail: info@futurekids.co.za
WWW address: http://www.futurekids.co.za

K-Net: learning to have fun

The 'K' in 'K-Net' stands not, as one might suspect, for kids. It stands for knowledge. What does knowledge stand for? Learning. Problem-solving. Lateral thinking. Coping with technology. But more than anything else, it stands for having fun.

'ComputerFun' is what they call it. For the more advanced, 'Techno-Fun'. Either way, it's an approach that puts the emphasis on learning how to use computers, rather than learning *about* computers.

'Who really cares about ROM and RAM and all that stuff?' shrugs Jill Hrdliczka, founder and managing director of the Gauteng-based group. 'What you need to know is what computers can do, and how they can make a difference to your life.'

To tell the truth, Jill does care a little about ROM and RAM and all that stuff. Principal of Damelin Computer School for four years, she brings a sound knowledge of computer science, theory and business to the arena of computer tutoring for kids.

Indeed, two of K-Net's four learning centres are based at schools (Krugersdorp High and St Peter's Preparatory), and the group offers a range of courses for 'anyone from 3 to 103'. Let's stick to the bottom end of that scale for now.

K-Net's approach to toddler tutoring is simple: Bring your parents. 'Kids that age can learn a lot from computers,' says Jill. 'But they're still too young to be comfortable around strangers. They can get very clingy and anxious, so we like to have a parent or two present. That way, everyone's involved in the process.'

Younger children are taught four to a class; older children, in groups of 6 to 12. One child per computer.

'We share ideas and we share knowledge,' says Jill. 'We don't share computers. Children enjoy learning and experiencing things on their own. If one wants to draw a blue sun, and one wants to draw a yellow sun, that's fine by us.'

Aside from artistic expression, K-Net's curriculum includes everything from desktop publishing to word processing to researching school projects on the Internet. For older children who want to learn about ROM and RAM and all that stuff, advanced courses are offered in computer upgrading and repair, Web site development, and programming with Visual Basic.

'We treat every lesson as a project, focusing on the end result rather than the mechanics of the medium. The brief might be, "Let's do a picture of an animal today." We'll load up a CD-ROM encyclopaedia, find our picture, copy it, paste it into a painting program, add our own background, and print it out. If we're learning to use a spreadsheet program, on the other hand, our project would be "How to Make a Million".'

Any guarantees? No, but there is this Standard 6 kid who put his K-Net computing skills to practical use by selling laser-printed study notes to his classmates. For the rest, having fun is reward enough.

Tel: (011) 803-5554
E-mail: knet@knet.co.za
WWW address: http://www.knet.co.za

Kids 2000: game for anything

Marcelle Steyn, working mother and computer programmer, made the mistake of taking her three-year-old son to the office one day. He drove her crazy. He drove the rest of the office crazy. Marcelle had no option.

'I sat him down in front of a computer, put his little hand on the mouse, and told him to keep himself busy for a while.' He did. Marcelle was amazed. 'He was moving the cursor around on the screen, pointing at pictures, dragging icons. And I'd never shown him a thing.' Something clicked. Result: Kids 2000.

Based on the upper level of a shopping centre in Bryanston, Marcelle's computer training centre sets out to put kids on the road to the New Millennium. They're in the driver's seat, and they know exactly where they're going.

'The big difference between kids and adults,' says Marcelle, 'is that kids don't associate computers with work. If they're sitting at a computer, whatever they're doing, they're playing a game. That's why they're able to absorb knowledge so much quicker.'

Kids 2000 follows a structured, 48-week training course, with modules ranging from freehand mouse-drawing for younger children, to PowerPoint presentations with sound and video for high schoolers. Given her background in software development, Marcelle also encourages more computer-savvy kids to try their hand at programming, although she admits: 'It's mostly a boy thing.'

She offers Internet training for children aged ten and older, and is reassuringly pragmatic on the issue of online safety.

'You can buy *Hustler* off the shelf, and you can get picked up on the street. You can't blame the Internet for everything. You've got to trust in your kids.'

More important, you've got to allow them to be kids. There's a world inside the computer, but there's a world beyond it too. Says Marcelle: 'If you're stealing time for kids to play on the computer, steal it from the TV. Not from playtime.'

Tel: (011) 706-7022
E-mail: kids2000@cis.co.za
WWW address: http://africa.cis.co.za:81/kids/clubs/kids2000/

Mouse Mates and Gecko Bytes: home is where the hard drive is

Baby crawls down the corridor. A ginger cat sneaks through the burglar-proofing. An ibis, interrupted during a routine inspection of the garden, takes flight with a squawk of protest. Inside, a three-year-old, made taller by a cushion borrowed from the couch, points at bouncing shapes on a computer screen.

'Red square. Yellow square. Blue circle. Green triangle.' It's a scene that could be echoed in hundreds of homes across the country, but this isn't just anybody's home. This is Mouse Mates.

Like many working mothers with a background in computing or education, Yvonne Booysen has found the ideal mix between suburban bliss and the challenges of life in the Global Village. With two Pentium multimedia systems set up in what used to be the 'sun room' of her house in Florida, Yvonne tutors computer kids aged three and up, running through a home-designed syllabus that covers everything from making fridge magnets to multimedia authoring.

It's a far cry from Yvonne's previous foray into information technology: data-processing and programming for the Edgars chain. No stranger to training grown-ups, Yvonne has learned that the usual rules don't apply when your students may not even be old enough to read.

'If you're training adults, you start with the basics of computing and work your way up. With kids, you start with what's on the screen, and you work your way outwards. The important thing is to make them feel at home with technology, and teach them a love of computing.'

Yvonne makes it easier by introducing an uncommon element to the equation: democracy.

'I allow each child to guide me according to what they enjoy doing most. Half the lesson will be taken up by a project, and then it'll be, "Where do you want to go today?"'

With projects that include 'Making a Mask', 'Designing a T-Shirt', and 'Sending a Fax to Dad', the answer is hardly ever 'home'.

Says Yvonne: 'I've never met a kid who isn't interested in computers. Some of them might be a little overawed at first, but there's always a line that they cross — and from that moment on, it's just totally "Wow!"'

The same applies at Gecko Bytes in Randpark Ridge, where high school teacher Kate Poole runs computer learning courses in a home-from-home environment. That means: more than just computers.

'Whether it's video games, computers or the Internet, today's kids are bombarded by audio-visual media wherever they go. We believe they should be encouraged to use their own imaginations and creative abilities as well.'

So, in-between the computer lessons, which are based on guidelines from South African pre- and junior primary education departments, the Gecko Byte kids take time to indulge in such hands-on activities as painting, pottery and interactive theatre. It's a balanced philosophy, designed to lead kids into the Digital Age, while making sure their interests remain rooted in the real world.

'Our goal is to make kids feel comfortable with computers,' says Kate. 'We're not trying to produce boffins who sit glued to their screens 24 hours a day.'

Kate's computer classes are limited to eight children at a time, paired to four Pentium computers. 'When you've got two kids sharing a PC, it's the most exciting thing. There's this buzz that runs through the classroom.'

Yes, but don't they fight over the mouse?

'That's an easy one to deal with,' says Kate. 'I go around the class saying, "You're the sun, you're the moon." And when the sun is up, the moon is sleeping.'

Mouse Mates Tel: (011) 672-8459
E-mail: abooysen@icon.co.za
WWW address: http://www.icon.co.za/~abooysen/
Gecko Bytes Tel: (011) 476-9614

How to speak cyber

A handy glossary for the older generation of newbies

There's probably nothing quite as uncool as a parent trying to sound as cool as a kid. But there's no harm in trying. Pepper your conversation with these computer-related terms, many of which have slipped into everyday usage, and your offspring are bound to be impressed. At least once they've stopped ROTFL. L8r, doodz.

404 (pronounced 'four-oh-four') One who is totally clueless, as in, 'Gee, Mom, you're so 404 when it comes to computers.' Comes from the familiar '404 Error' generated by a Web site that is no longer in existence.

Analogue A member of the pre-digital generation, as in, 'My Dad's such an analogue — he still sends letters by post.'

Beta The pre-release version of a software package, usually riddled with bugs. Can also be applied to other areas of life, as in, 'Here's my trigonometry assignment, Miss. I must warn you that it's still in Beta.'

Bithead One who spends an inordinate amount of time connected to a computer or the Net. Not to be confused, except in extreme cases, with 'butt-head'.

Bug A form of artificial but highly intelligent life that climbs inside a computer and makes it not work. Many people believe that Windows 95 is actually a bug.

THE PC PARENT

Bells and Whistles Extraneous hardware or software features, designed to fool people into thinking you are intimately acquainted with digital technology. A fine example would be a telephone handset connected to your computer monitor.

Cheat codes Simple but ostensibly top-secret commands that allow you to play a computer game without having to do any thinking. Warning, kids: Playing computer games all day can seriously jeopardise your chances of passing matric. Unless you get the cheat codes.

Clicker-happy Behaviour of a juvenile whose parents have just bought him a computer with a modem, and who is trying to make up for lost time by clicking every link on the World Wide Web.

Crack A small program, usually distributed on the Internet, that allows you to bypass the security features and limitations of a shareware or demonstration program. Illegal, of course, but what does that mean on the Internet?

Crash A major system malfunction that could take weeks — not to mention geeks — to repair. Traditionally occurs on the night before a homework assignment is due.

Cutting-edge Hot-off-the-conveyer-belt technology or thinking that will be obsolete in three weeks' time.

Cyberia Where your kids go when you banish them from using the Internet.

Cyberspace The Internet. A once cutting-edge term, now used only by newbies and authors of computer books. Everyone else just says 'The Net'.

Dead tree edition The foldable version of a newspaper or magazine that is also available on the World Wide Web.

Defrag To attempt to get one's life into some semblance of order, usually on 1 January. From the practice of 'defragmenting' a computer's hard drive to reorganise the data and improve performance. As in, 'Sorry, I can't make it to the rave on Saturday. I've got to stay home and defrag.'

De-lurk To re-enter a discussion, usually on an Internet newsgroup, after a long period of self-enforced inactivity. Can also be applied to teenagers who suddenly spring to life when the dinner-table conversation turns to washing-up. *See also* **Lurk**.

Doodz Dudes who can't, or more likely won't, spell.

Dub World Wide Web location, from 'WWW'. As in, 'You're on the Web? Gimme your dub, man!'

Edutainment The practice of educating your children by stealth, or entertaining them with an easy conscience.

Eye candy A Web site or software package that is stronger on visual appeal than substance. Can also be applied to Pamela Anderson.

FUD Fear, Uncertainty and Doubt — the trinity of terrifying emotions that accompany any new venture into the minefield of personal computing. As in, 'Weighed down with FUD and money, I set out to buy a Pentium multimedia system for my kids.'

Geek One who is intimately acquainted with the ins and outs of computer technology. Usually a male.

God mode A position of acquired invincibility in a computer game. Can also be applied to certain schoolmasters and politicians.

Hard copy The printed version of stuff that otherwise exists only inside a computer or on the Internet. It is a good principle not to believe anything you read until you see it in hard copy.

Irritainment A program or Web site that is supposed to be edutaining, but only succeeds in driving you up the wall.

Kewl Cooler than cool. Not for use by parents, except in emergencies.

Leeching Borrowing ideas or information from the Internet without acknowledgement or attribution. Also common in secondary education circles, as in, 'Mind if I leech your Maths homework before class?'

L8r A more cost-effective way of saying 'See you later' in e-mail.

Lurk To be affirmatively inactive in cyberspace. Lurkers are commonplace on Internet newsgroups, where they silently digest raging discussions until they can think of something interesting to say.

Matrix A more impressive-sounding term for the Internet. As in, 'Sorry, Mom, I can't come to supper right now. I'm on the Matrix.'

Millennium Rush The terrifying, head-pounding feeling associated with the knowledge that the New Millennium is just around the corner, and you haven't got a thing to wear.

Mouse potato Someone who used to be a couch potato, until his parents decided to buy him a computer.

Multi-mediocrity A multimedia program that doesn't quite live up to expectations.

Nerdling An aspirant nerd. As in, 'Shame. The poor nerdling was trying to play *Quake* on his old man's 386.'

Netiquette The rigidly applied code of conduct that allows you to unleash a tirade of obscene and abusive language on an Internet newsgroup, as long as you don't use CAPITAL LETTERS.

Newbie One who is still feeling his or her way around the Internet. To call someone a newbie on a public forum is a sure sign that you are a newbie.

Ohnosecond The amount of time it takes to realise you've done something drastically wrong, and it is too late to undo it. As in, 'Man, I just hit the enter key, and in less than an ohnosecond, I'd reformatted my hard drive.'

Outernet The furthest fringes of the Internet, where the kooks, crazies, weirdos, psychos, hackers, crackers and your teenage children like to hang out.

Phreaking Using high technology or inside knowledge to make free calls from a public phonebox. Not to be confused with 'freaking', which is what parents do when they find out.

ROTFL Rolling on the Floor with Laughter. Internet acronym, usually abbreviated to 'Roll!' in real life. As in, 'My folks bought me a multi-media computer so I could improve my marks.' 'Roll!'

Schlurf To attempt to surf the Internet when the Americans are hogging all the bandwidth, usually between 3 pm and midnight South African time. Cross between surf and schlepp.

Snail-mail Non-electronic mail. Rarely used nowadays, except to send cheques.

Scrolling The ability to absorb information without actually ingesting it. From the Internet practice of scrolling through large chunks of text in the hope of encountering something interesting. As in, 'Did you study for your Biology exam?' 'Of course, Dad, I was up scrolling all night long.'

Spam Malicious or useless e-mail that clogs up your system. Often hard to tell apart from the other e-mail that clogs up your system.

Surf What people who live on the coast go out and do while waiting for their Web pages to load.

Virtual An experience or sensation that is so unreal, it's almost real. As in, 'Can I go to the rave tonight, Mom? I've virtually finished my homework.'

Warez Pirated commercial software distributed on the Internet by individuals who believe all information should be free.

Y2K The year 2000, which we will hopefully be able to stop calling 'the year 2000' in the year 2000.

Index

3-D Ultra Pinball 85, 93
3D Movie Maker 70, 75, 100
101 Dalmations Animated Storybook 90
123 Foo

A
accessories 13
Acer 18, 19
A.D.A.M., The Inside Story 74
Afrikaanse Hoërskool Sasolburg 189
Alfoobet 84
AltaVista 129, 132–3
Amy's Fun 2–3 Adventure 81
Animated Clock 83
Apple Macintosh 16, 40, 69
APS 25
arts and crafts 82–3
Auwa 20

B
B.J.'s Pinchbeck's Homework Helper 146–7
Baby Keys 81
background 162, 163
backing up 21, 25
backward-compatibility 69
Barbie 95, 97, 100, 123
Barbie Fashion Designer 96, 100
Battle Chess 169
BlackBox Math Expert 83
blink rates 92
blocking programs 108–14, 178
Bobby's First Letters 82
bookmark 140, 141, 156
Boolean Operators 133–4
brand-names 18, 19, 20, 77
byte 20

C
careware 78
Carmen Sandiego 95, 97
Carpal Tunnel Syndrome 36, 50, 52
Castle Infinity 84
CatMinus for Windows 81
CD-ROM 28, 38, 45, 65, 68, 72, 73, 95, 96, 98, 108, 170, 173, 187, 204, 205; drive 13, 16, 17, 22, 24, 45, 46, 48, 191; encyclopaedia 169, 192, 198
censorship 112
central file server 169
central processing unit (CPU) 18, 20
chairs 51–2

chat forums 184
child development 28
Child's Play II 82
childproofing 42–9
Children's Multimedia Encyclipaedia 73
clicking 16, 37, 41, 52, 178, 205
clones 18, 19, 20
COBOL 169
collaborative learning 205, 206
Comfy Keyboard 32, 33
commercial demons 84–6
communication skills 178, 184
Compaq 18, 19
computer centre 206; checklist for 173–4
computer chip, *see* central processing unit
computer literacy 30, 135, 169, 173, 174, 178
computer publications 67, 79
computing skills 70, 184, 204, 205, 208
copyright 192
Corel Photo-Paint 60
Corel PrintHouse 73
CorelDRAW 6 60
CorelDRAW 7 60
crawler, *see* search engine
Crayola Art Studio 76
Creative Writer 85
crippleware 78
Cronicle of the 20th Century 76
Curriculum 2005 172
cursor control 37, 38, 39, 70
CuteFTP 159
Cyber Patrol 109–10, 113
Cyber Snoop 112
CyberGladiators 85, 96, 100
Cybersitter 110–1, 113
CyberSky 84
CyberTaxi 116

D
dangers 114
database management 208
defining 131, 134
Deja News 140
demoware 78, 94
desktop publishing 210
Diablo 56, 93
display card, *see* video card
Dogpile 137, 141
Doodle's Graphics Directory 162
Doom II 90
Doom 33, 88, 90, 91, 93, 192

Dorling Kindersley 70, 74, 75, 76
DOS 16, 59, 69, 79, 81, 83, 205;
 compatibility 17
double-clicking 70
downloading 80, 94, 163
Dr Seuss's ABC 74
Dr Seuss 85
dragging 178, 205
DRAM 21
Duke Nukem 3D 88, 89, 91, 92

E
e-mail 24, 59, 99, 112, 139, 140, 158, 160, 168,
 169, 170, 175, 176, 180, 181, 184, 186,
 217, 220
Ecola's Newsstand 141
Edmark 84
edutainment 22, 65–75, 217
Electronic Geoboard 84
Enchanted Forest 159
encouragement 31, 72
English, use of 69–70
epilepsy 91
Epson 24
ergonomics 40, 51
Evil House of Cheat 195
Excite 129
'exe' extension 80
experts 142, 184
eyestrain 53–4
Eyewitness Encyclopaedia of Science 74

F
Farnsworth Ferret's Fun Pack 81
FAQ, *see* frequently-asked question
feedback 31, 72
File Transfer Protocol (FTP) 80, 112, 159,
 196; client 81, 159
files: backing up 47–8; password protection
 49, 113; Read-Only protection 49;
 safeguarding 47–9
floppy disk 44
floppy-disk drive 14, 46
Foo Castle 84
freeware 78
frequently-asked question (FAQ) 15, 142
FTP, *see* File Transfer Protocol
Fujitsu 18, 19
furnishings 206
Futurekids 204, 205, 206, 207–9

G
Gabriel Knight II: The Beast Within 93
games 22, 24, 28, 56, 57, 59, 65, 72, 84, 87–94,
 110, 168, 178, 208, 217

Gecko Bytes 211–3
Geocities 159
gigabyte 20
gimmicks 73
Girl Games 97
girls 95–100
GirlTech 97
Goosebumps: Escape from Horrorland 94
government legislation 113
Graphic User Interface 29
graphics 36, 56, 57, 60, 96, 153, 156, 162, 163,
 187, 191, 208
graphics card, *see* video card
Graphmatic 83
Greatest Paper Airplanes 84
Greetings Workshop 76
Grolier Multimedia Encyclopaedia 67
group interaction 174
Gryphon Bricks 85
Gryphon Software 85

H
hand–eye co-ordination 92
hard disk, *see* hard drive
hard drive 16, 19, 20, 21, 23, 46, 68, 77, 187,
 216
hardware 19, 43, 68, 148, 178, 207
hate speech 111
health 50–4, 91–2
Her Interactive 97
Hewlett Packard 24
High Times 111
hobbies 84
home page 67, 177; how to build 148–66;
 tips for designing 161–2;
 free items 162–7
Home Page Creation Centre, The 163
homeschooling 197–203; sites on the
 Internet 203
Homeschooling Zone 203
homework 56, 58, 146, 169, 191–8, 209
Homework Homepage, The 195
HotBot 129, 132
HotDog Pro 154
HotMetal Pro 154
HotSprings 159
HTML, *see* Hypertext Markup Language
hyperlink 140, 157, 160, 161, 176
Hypertext Markup Language (HTML) 153–4,
 156, 187; editing program 147, 154, 161,
 187; file 155, 188; special effects 158
hypertext reference 157

I
icon 162

Icon Department, The 162
Incredible Machine, The 85
Independent Online 139
information-gathering skills 104, 135, 140, 152, 194
information, sharing of 192
Infoseek Guide 129, 131–2, 135
InfoSpace 160
inkjet printer, *see* printer
installation process 80
integration 178
interaction 32, 33, 35, 72
Interactive Dental Office 83
interactive: education 39; edutainment 65; software 38
Internet connection 173
Internet Explorer 113, 141
Internet Relay Chat (IRC) 104, 110, 112
Internet service provider (ISP) 20, 23, 108, 158, 159, 160
Internet, the 13, 15, 19, 20, 23, 36, 49, 55, 57, 58, 59, 67, 77, 80, 94, 98, 100–63, 168, 170, 172, 175–85, 200, 203, 207, 208, 210, 212, 216, 217, 218, 220
Interplay 85
Introducing kids to computers 26–34
Iomega Zip 100 25, 48
ISP, *see* Internet service provider

J
Jackson's Page for Five Year Olds 152
Jeppe Boys' High School 189
Jon's Homeschool Resource Page 203
joystick 24, 52, 96
JumpStart Toddlers 74
Just Grandma and Me 32, 37, 70, 74
Just Me and My Dad 35

K
K-Net 55, 59, 206, 209–10
Kai's Power Goo 75
Kasparov's Gambit 94
Kensington mouse 39
keyboard 21, 23, 31, 33, 42, 45, 46, 47, 52, 53, 71, 92, 135
keyword 131, 133
Kid CAD 73
Kid Pix Studio 75
Kid's Typing 76
Kids 2000 210–11
KidPix 100
kilobytes 23, 80
Kloofwaters Intermediate School 189
Koala Kid, The 149–53
Krush Kill 'n' Destroy 50, 97

L
laptop 31, 41, 116
laser printer, *see* printer
Lawrence Goetz's Home Page 79
learning 81, 92–3
Learning in Toyland 74
Lenny's Toons 68
Let's Talk about Me 98
Level 2 (L2) memory 20, 23
Leximark 24
lighting 51, 91
Lil' Picasso 82–3
links 133, 135, 141, 161, 163
Lion King, The 65, 123
Logitech: Kidz Mouse 40; WingMan 25
Looksmart 129
Lycos Pictures and Sounds Directory 141

M
Maddy's Mayhem 100% Fun! Page 152
Magellan 129
magic Folders 49
Magic School Bus 85
Mail & Guardian 139
mainframe 169
Mario Teaches Typing 85
Math Blaster 75, 92
Math Shareware and Freeware 80
maths 83
matrix 218
McKenzie & Me 98
MetaCrawler 129
megabyte 20, 80
memory 19, 68
Mercer 25
MetaSearch 141
microprocessor 169
Microscope 83
Microsoft 85, 94; Backup Utility 48; *Bugs* 57; compatible mouse 24; Diagnostics 69; *Dinosaurs* 75; EasyBall 40; *Encarta* 58, 69, 73, 74, 108, 191, 192; *Flight Simulator* 94; Home Mouse 39; Natural Keyboard 21; PowerPoint 60, 170, 211; *Publisher* 85; Sidewinder 3-D 25; Word 49, 60
MIDI sound 153
Millie's Math House 81
MineraLogic 83
modem 13, 22, 24, 103, 109, 133, 176, 184, 207, 216
monitor 46, 51, 52, 53, 54, 91, 92; anti-glare 53; SVGA 16, 23
Monster Truck Madness 94
Mortal Kombat 88
motherboard 16

mouse 16, 21–22, 31, 35–41, 52, 66, 70, 92, 103, 156, 178, 205, 211; tips for using 40–1
Mouse Mates 211–3
mousepad 39
multimedia 22, 68, 70, 136, 187, 206, 208, 211, 212; computer 15, 16, 20, 43, 46, 108, 168, 171, 191; software 13, 22, 63–100, 218; upgrade kit 68
multitasking 29, 192
Muppet Treasure Island 56
Mustek 24
My First Amazing, Incredible Dictionary 38, 74
Myst 89

N
nagware 78
Nando Times 139
national schools' network 182
nausea 91
Need for Speed 94
NerdWorld 160
Net Nanny 109, 113
Netscape 178
netiquette 218
News Reader 107
newsgroup 104, 109, 112, 137, 139, 140, 170, 175, 184, 203, 216, 217
Nickelodeon 3D Movie Maker 85
Norton Backup for Windows 48
Notepad 154, 155
nudity 113

O
O'Connor House Software 84
online library 183
online newspapers and magazines 139, 140, 141
online resources 183
online technical support 77

P
Pac-Man 87
packaging 66, 77
Packard Bell 18, 19
parental guidance 111
parents 93–4
PASCAL 169
password-protection 90
PC Pals Mouse 'n House 40
PCI VGA card 23
Pentium 16, 18, 20, 55, 59, 66, 168, 197, 211, 212; II 20; MMX 20; Pro 20; processor 23
Performa 17, 18
PF Magic 85

Phantasmagoria 88, 90
plagiarism 156, 162
Plug and Play 17, 19
Pointcast 109
Pong 87
pornography 103, 104, 106, 108
postcardware 78
posture 52
power supply 25
PowerPC chip 18
price 14, 68, 77
printers: 45, 205, 207; colour injet 24, 173, 207; laser 173
private tutition 204–13
problem-solving 72
processor 16, 19
programming 57, 100, 210, 211
Putt-Putt Goes to the Moon 75
Putt-Putt's Adventure to Mavis Beacon's Typing Tutor 68
Putt-Putt 85

R
Random Access Memory (RAM) 16, 20, 23, 56, 61, 209, 210
rating system 113, 114
Recreational Software Advisory Council (RSAC) 90
refining 131, 133, 134
removable storage device 25
Repetitive Strain Injury (RSI) 52, 92
research 131, 184, 192, 193, 210
Research Papers Online 193, 196
robot, *see* search engine
Rocket Download 79

S
SafeSurf Council 113
safety 45–6, 50–4
scanners 24, 45, 57, 173, 207
School Is Dead, Learn in Freedom! Page 203
School Sucks 193, 196
schools 57, 59, 92, 165–213, 175–9
science 83
screen, *see* monitor
search engines 110, 128–31, 132, 133, 135, 137, 138, 141, 142, 197
searching 131; tips for 140–2
second-hand computer 15
secondary cache, *see* Level 2 memory
setting out and starting up 13–25
shareware 49, 77–86, 163, 216; where to find 79–80
Shareware.com 79
'shift-and-lift' method 38

Show and Tell 82
Sierra Online 85
SimCity 85, 89, 169
single-clicking 70
Snakes 84
social interaction skills 206
software 17, 19, 20, 22, 24, 28, 32, 41, 43, 63–100, 108, 149, 169, 171, 178, 187, 188, 207, 208, 214, 217;
    how to choose and buy 65–75
Soleil Software 85
Sound Blaster 22, 24
sound cards 22, 65, 156
South African College High School 189
So You Want to Make a Web Page! 154
Space Invaders 14, 87
spelling 161
spreadsheet 48, 55, 173, 191
St David's Marist College 189
St Stithians College 189
Star, The 140
Stevie's Graphics, Pictures and Sounds 162
stiffy disk 22, 44, 46, 79
stiffy drive 21, 23
Storybook Weaver 73, 100
sums and numbers 81–2
SunsetStrip 159
supervision 28, 43–4, 178
SurfWatch 111–2

T
tags 154, 155, 156, 157, 158, 163
teachers 58, 60, 172, 173, 175, 179, 180–5, 198, 205, 207
technology 172, 173, 180, 184, 187, 204, 208, 209, 212, 216
Technology-Based Learning Centre Education 172
Teen Movie Critic 149–53, 200
tele-access 183
tele-monitoring 184
tele-presence 183–4
tele-publishing 184
tele-sharing 184
Term Papers for Free 196
Tetris 98, 100
The Edutainment Company 85
Tigger's Home 80
TrueSpace 60
TurboCAD 73
tutor checklist 206–7
typing 56, 59, 68
Typing Attack 59

U
Ultimate Human Body, The 75
Ultimate Language Tutor 82
Umax 24
upgrading 22, 77
uploading 155
Usenet 67, 110, 137, 140, 175, 203

V
VDT glasses 54
video 103, 124, 211; card 19, 21
Video Game-Related Seizure (VGRS) 91
violence 89–90, 111, 113
virtual reality 91
vision 91
Visual Basic 55, 57, 59, 61, 210
Vividus Software 86
VRAM 21

W
Way Things Work, The 74
Web annoucement service 160
Web browser 107, 112, 113, 115, 127, 154, 155, 161, 187
Web server 159
Web spider, *see* search engine
Web Wizard, The 163
Web Workshop 86
WebThing 154
Weekly Speller 82
Westerford High School 190
What's New listing 160
What's New Too 160
Where in the World is Carmen Sandiego? 75, 92, 95
wildcards 141
Windows 3.1 40, 48, 69, 79, 80, 81, 82, 83, 84, 110, 163, 177, 187
Windows 95 17, 19, 20, 41, 48, 61, 69, 79, 80, 81, 82, 83, 84, 86, 110, 112, 163, 187, 205
WinSite Archive 79
WinZip 80
word processor 170, 207, 208, 210
Word Wrestle 82
words and letters 82
World Wide Web 52, 79, 80, 94, 96, 115–26, 135, 136, 146, 148, 149, 150, 152, 154, 169, 175, 176, 178, 180, 181, 186–90, 210, 216, 217, 220; schools on the 188–90
World Walker 85
Wrestlemania 89
Wykeham College, The 190

Y
Yahoo Image Surfer 141
Yahoo! 129
Yahooligans! 129
Yikes! 163

Z
ZDNet Software Library 79
'zip' file extension 80
Zurk's Learning Safari 85
Zurk's Rainforest Lab 85